Praise for *Reformed Theology from A to Z*

"What a useful resource! From busy pastors in need of a quick reference to students just digging into a particular topic, all will appreciate Don McKim's informed and accessible introduction to the names, terms, and concerns of the Reformed faith."— **Kenneth J. Woo**, Pittsburgh Theological Seminary

"Donald McKim has done it again! With his characteristic mixture of perceptive scholarship and accessible prose, McKim has crafted a guide to key concepts, figures, and controversies in Reformed theology throughout its history. A much-needed, reader-friendly reference work and introduction to a rich theological tradition." —**David H. Jensen**, professor in the Clarence N. and Betty B. Frierson distinguished chair of reformed theology, Austin Presbyterian Theological Seminary

"This handy guidebook provides an accessible entrance into Reformed theology for students, church folks, and general readers who want an introduction to basic terms in this Christian family. Strongly recommended for all classes in Reformed theology!" —**Martha Moore-Keish**, J.B. Green professor of theology, Columbia Theological Seminary

"Donald McKim is a premier encyclopedist and this subject is his specialty. I highly recommend this as a reference work for all students in the field." —**Michael S. Horton**, J. Gresham Machen Professor, Westminster Seminary California

Reformed Theology from A to Z

Donald K. McKim

ROWMAN & LITTLEFIELD
Lanham • Boulder • New York • London

Published by Rowman & Littlefield
An imprint of The Rowman & Littlefield Publishing Group, Inc.
4501 Forbes Boulevard, Suite 200, Lanham, Maryland 20706
www.rowman.com

86-90 Paul Street, London EC2A 4NE

British Library Cataloguing in Publication Information Available

Library of Congress Cataloging-in-Publication Data

Names: McKim, Donald K., author.
Title: Reformed theology from A to Z / Donald K. McKim.
Description: Lanham : Rowman & Littlefield, [2023] | Includes
  bibliographical references and index.
Identifiers: LCCN 2023011013 (print) | LCCN 2023011014 (ebook) | ISBN
  9781538176771 (cloth) | ISBN 9781538176788 (paperback) | ISBN
  9781538176795 (ebook)
Subjects: LCSH: Reformed Church—Theology. | Theology—Terminology. |
  Theology—Dictionaries.
Classification: LCC BX9406 .M39 2023 (print) | LCC BX9406 (ebook) |
  DDC 284/.2—dc23/eng/20230601
LC record available at https://lccn.loc.gov/2023011013
LC ebook record available at https://lccn.loc.gov/2023011014

To Jim West—my friend, coauthor, and fellow theologian,
whose life is devoted to glorifying
and serving God—with great gratitude

Contents

x ～ Contents

~

Preface

I was delighted when my friend and former colleague Richard Brown, senior executive editor for religion at Rowman & Littlefield, mentioned an interesting book he was reading that had "A to Z" in its title. The book provided short discussions of the topic in a concise manner. Richard wondered if some book(s) with this concept could be written in the field of religion. I thought: What about *Reformed Theology from A to Z*?

I have spent my life thinking and writing about Reformed theology for various audiences and through different approaches. It has been my joy! So I was eager to take up the task of providing short discussions of important terms in Reformed theology. With tons of writings already available on these terms in the works of major theologians and heavy-duty theological books and articles, it was a challenge to try to capture the major dimensions of each term and to write about it in three hundred words. My hope is that this distillation is accurate and will introduce readers to major aspects of the terms in a clear way. Then—I hope!—the next step will be for readers to find other theological works that will further enhance understandings of these theological concepts.

I trust such an A-to-Z treatment in this fashion will have its place. I hope this book will be helpful to beginning theological students, to pastors, and to those who are interested in theology but need a gentle way to get acquainted with terms that are the building blocks of Reformed theology.

Throughout, I have mentioned major theologians whose works provide more detailed discussions of these theological terms. A source I use often here is the *Book of Confessions* of the Presbyterian Church in the United States of America (PC[USA]). I am ordained in this denomination, and its collection of confessional statements from the early church to the present day, which serves as the denomination's doctrinal standards, is a most convenient source for Reformed theology.[1]

I am most grateful to Richard Brown for his interest in this project and for planting the seed of the initial idea from which this book has grown. Our friendship and our previous publishing work together is one of my true enjoyments. I thank Richard for his support, past and present.

I dedicate this book to my friend Jim West. Jim is a biblical and Reformation scholar and pastor with whom I have written several books on Protestant reformers: *Heinrich Bullinger: An Introduction to His Life and Theology* (Cascade, 2022), *Martin Bucer: An Introduction to His Life and Theology* (Cascade, 2023), and *Theodore Beza: An Introduction to His Life and Theology* (Cascade, forthcoming). Our collaboration has been wonderful. Jim's humor leavens all we do, and his scholarly competence is so helpful for our common work. I am very thankful to and for Jim!

My family provides the context for all I try to do as a theologian and a person. My wife, LindaJo, is my light and joy. I cannot express how grateful I am for her love and our life together. We are blessed by our sons and their families: Stephen and Caroline and their children, Maddie, Annie, Jack, and Ford; and Karl and Lauren. They bring happiness to us—without measure!

This book is offered to all who would learn of Reformed theology—a theology that seeks "to do everything for the glory of God" (1 Cor. 10:31). As we study theology, may all of us find, as the Reformed theologian William Ames put it, "Theology is the doctrine or teaching [*doctrina*] of living to God." As Ames wrote, "Since the highest kind of life for a human being is that which approaches most closely the living and life-giving God, the nature of theological life is living to God" (*Marrow*, 77). May we so live!

Donald K. McKim

Note

1. *The Book of Confessions* is available in print form from the PC(USA) store: https://www.pcusastore.com/Products/0664262902/book-of-confessions-study-edition-revised.aspx. It is also available as a free download under "The Book of Confessions" at https://oga.pcusa.org/section/mid-council-ministries/constitutional-services/constitution/#confessions.

Christmas 2022

~

Introduction

This book is a gateway to Reformed theology. Here you will find short discussions of terms that are important in this major branch of Christian theology. This is a theology with a tradition that stretches back to the sixteenth-century Protestant Reformation period. Reformed theology, as it developed, was distinct from Lutheran theology, which emerged through the work of Martin Luther (1483–1546), Philip Melanchthon (1497–1560), and other Protestant reformers. Reformed theology looks back to the work of John Calvin (1509–1564), Huldrych Zwingli (1484–1531), and others, who developed theological concepts they believed were consistent with the Scriptures and could be reliable guides for what Christians can believe and indicate how God wants them to live.

Reformed theology has lived—and continues to live—in Reformed churches. The World Communion of Reformed Churches (WCRC) was formed in 2010 as a successor to the World Alliance of Reformed Churches (1875). The Communion is "comprised of 100 million Christians in Congregational, Presbyterian, Reformed, United, Uniting and Waldensian churches. The WCRC, working with its 233 member churches, is active in supporting theology, justice, church unity and mission in over 105 countries" (http://wcrc.ch/about-us).

In North America, Reformed churches are comprised of denominations aligned as Presbyterian, Congregational, European Reformed,

Reformed Baptist, Reformed Charismatic, Uniting and United, and others. Among the largest denominations are the Presbyterian Church in the United States of America, the United Church of Christ (UCC), and the United Church of Canada. There are more than 6 million Presbyterians in North America (https://en.wikipedia.org/wiki /List_of_Presbyterian_and_Reformed_denominations_in_North _America#Uniting_and_United_denominations).

In the United States, prominent Reformed denominations are the PC(USA), the UCC, the Presbyterian Church in America (PCA), Evangelical Presbyterian Church (EPC), and the ECO: Covenant Order of Evangelical Presbyterians (see *R&E*, appendix 1). Historic Reformed bodies in the Dutch Reformed denominations in the United States include the Reformed Church in America (RCA) and the Christian Reformed Church (CRC).

Reformed theology features many theological terms. Some of these are familiar to many Christians. Others represent more technical ideas. The goal of this book is to provide a pathway through theological terms as they are understood by Reformed theologians and in the documents—such as textbooks and Confessions of Faith—that are part of the Reformed theological tradition.

The terms move from "Accommodation" to "Zwinglianism"— literally from A to Z. Along the way, various theological sources are cited. These help to explain the terms and also indicate sources where each theological concept is discussed more fully. Full source citations for the references are found in the Sources Cited list. To encourage further study, the Annotated Bibliography lists works that provide fuller understandings of Reformed theology. A short description indicates features of these works.

The hope is that this A-to-Z guide will be a ready reference when one reads or hears a theological term and seeks further understanding. The articles here cover *main* dimensions of the terms; the need for further discussion of the terms and the issues they address is apparent.

So these short introductions to the terms are truly entry points. They are meant to encourage further study and further understanding of the richness—and ongoing importance—of Reformed theology. An asterisk after a word indicates that this particular term is defined elsewhere in the book.

~

Sources Cited

BC   *Book of Confessions*, Study Edition Revised. Louisville,
              KY: Westminster John Knox Press, 2017. Avail-
              able as a free download: https://oga.pcusa.org/section
              /mid-council-ministries/constitutional-services
              /constitution

BO   *The Book of Order*. Presbyterian Church in the USA.
              Available as a free download: https://oga.pcusa.org/sec
              tion/mid-council-ministries/constitutional-services
              /constitution

Breastplate   Preston, John. *The Breastplate of Faith and Love*. Lon-
              don, 1651.

Calvinism   Hart, D. G. *Calvinism: A History*. New Haven, CT:
              Yale University Press, 2013.

CCT   Holder, R. Ward. *Calvin and the Christian Tradition:
              Scripture, Memory, and the Western Mind*. New York:
              Cambridge University Press, 2022.

CD   Barth, Karl. *Church Dogmatics*. Trans. G. W. Bromi-
              ley, T. F. Torrance, and others. 13 vols. Edinburgh:
              T&T Clark, 1936–1969.

CF   Schleiermacher, Friedrich. *Christian Faith: A New Translation and Critical Edition*. 2 vols. Ed. Catherine L. Kelsey and Terrence N. Tice. Trans. Terrence N. Tice, Catherine L. Kelsey, and Edwina Lawler. Louisville, KY: Westminster John Knox Press, 2016.

Church   Moltmann, Jürgen. *The Church in the Power of the Spirit: A Contribution to Messianic Ecclesiology*. New York: Harper & Row, 1977.

"Clarity and   "Of the Clarity and Certainty or Power of the Word
Certainty"   of God." In *Zwingli and Bullinger*. Ed. and trans. G. W. Bromiley. Library of Christian Classics. Philadelphia: Westminster Press, 1953.

CNTC   Calvin's New Testament Commentaries. Ed. David W. Torrance and Thomas F. Torrance. 12 vols. Grand Rapids, MI: William B. Eerdmans.

Coming   Moltmann, Jürgen. *The Coming of God: Christian Eschatology*. Trans. Margaret Kohl. Minneapolis: Fortress Press, 1996.

Common Places   Bucer, Martin. *Common Places of Martin Bucer*. Ed. David F. Wright. Abingdon, UK: Sutton Courtenay Press, 1972.

Creation   Christian Reformed Church. "Creation Care and Climate Justice." https://www.crcna.org/SocialJustice/creation-care-climate-justice

CRO   *A Companion to Reformed Orthodoxy*. Ed. Herman J. Selderhuis. Brill's Companions to the Christian Tradition. Boston: Brill, 2013.

Crucified   Moltmann, Jürgen. *The Crucified God*. Rpt. San Francisco: HarperSanFrancisco, 1991.

Decades   Bullinger, Heinrich. *Decades*. Available online at https://www.prdl.org/author_view.php?a_id=175

DLGTT   Muller, Richard A. *Dictionary of Latin and Greek Theological Terms: Drawn Principally from Protestant Scholastic Theology*. Grand Rapids, MI: Baker Book House, 1985.

Dort   *The Canons of Dort*. Christian Reformed Church, 2011.
             Available online at https://www.crcna.org/welcome
             /beliefs/confessions/canons-dort

DW   "Directory for Worship." In *The Book of Order*. Pres-
             byterian Church in the USA, 2019–2021. Available
             under "The Book of Order" at https://oga.pcusa.org
             /section/mid-council-ministries/constitutional
             -services/constitution

EE   Barth, Karl. *The Epistle to the Ephesians*. Ed. R. David
             Nelson. Trans. Ross M. Wright. Grand Rapids, MI:
             Baker Academic, 2017.

Engagement   Christian Reformed Church. "Reformed Christian
             Engagement with People of Other Faith." https://
             www.crcna.org/eirc/interfaith-relations/reformed
             -christian-engagement-people-different-faith

Equity   Haas, Guenther H. *The Concept of Equity in Calvin's
             Ethics*. Waterloo, ON: Wilfrid Laurier University
             Press, 1997.

ERF   McKim, Donald K., ed., *Encyclopedia of the Reformed
             Faith*. Louisville, KY: Westminster John Knox Press,
             1992.

Experiences Moltmann, Jürgen. *Experiences of God*. Trans. Marga-
             ret Kohl. Philadelphia: Fortress Press, 1980.

Faith   Barth, Karl. *The Faith of the Church: A Commentary on
             the Apostles' Creed According to Calvin's Catechism*. Ed.
             Jean-Louis Leuba. Trans. Gabriel Vahanian. Cleve-
             land, OH: World Publishing, 1959.

Faith Seeking Migliore, Daniel L. *Faith Seeking Understanding: An
             Introduction to Christian Theology*. Grand Rapids, MI:
             William B. Eerdmans, 2004.

Fragments   Barth, Karl. *Fragments Grave and Gay*. Ed. Martin
             Rumscheidt. Trans. Eric Mosbacher. London: Collins,
             1971.

GMG   Tipton, Stephen B. *The Ground, Method, and Goal of
                Amandus Polanus' (1561–1610) Doctrine of God: A
                Historical and Contextual Analysis.* Reformed Histori-
                cal Theology, vol. 73. Göttingen: Vandenhoeck &
                Ruprecht, 2022.

HCT   Barth, Karl. *The Heidelberg Catechism for Today.*
                Trans. Shirley C. Guthrie Jr. Richmond, VA: John
                Knox Press, 1964.

HKBCMM   McKim, Donald K., ed. *How Karl Barth Changed My
                Mind.* Grand Rapids, MI: William B. Eerdmans, 1986.

Holy Scripture Bloesch, Donald G. *Holy Scripture.* Christian Founda-
                tions. 7 vols. Downers Grove, IL: InterVarsity Press,
                1994.

Homiletic   Buttrick, David. *Homiletic: Moves and Structures.*
                Philadelphia: Fortress Press, 1987.

Inst.   Calvin, John. *Institutes of the Christian Religion.* Ed.
                John T. McNeill. Trans. Ford Lewis Battles. 2 vols.
                The Library of Christian Classics. Philadelphia: West-
                minster Press, 1960.

ISBE   *The International Standard Bible Encyclopedia.* Ed.
                James Orr. 5 vols. Chicago: Howard-Severance, 1915.

John Knox   Percy, Eustace. *John Knox.* London: Hodder, 1937.

Knowledge   Barth, Karl. *The Knowledge of God and the Service of
                God.* Trans. J. L. M. Haire and Ian Henderson. New
                York: Scribner's Sons, 1939.

Landmark   *A Landmark in Turbulent Times: The Meaning and
                Relevance of the Synod of Dordt (1618–1619).* Ed.
                Henk van den Belt, Klaas-Willem de Jong, Willem
                van Vlastuin. Refo500 Academic Studies. Göttingen:
                Vandenhoeck & Ruprecht, 2022.

LW   *Luther's Works,* vol. 25. St. Louis, MO: Concordia
                Publishing House, 1972.

Marrow   Ames, William. *The Marrow of Theology.* Trans. John
                Dykstra Eusden. Boston: Pilgrim Press, 1968.

Minutes — *Minutes of the General Assembly of the Presbyterian Church in the United States of America*. Philadelphia, 1910.

Mystery — Cochrane, Arthur. C. *The Mystery of Peace*. Elgin, IL: Brethren Press, 1986.

OHKB — *The Oxford Handbook of Karl Barth*. Ed. Paul Dafydd Jones and Paul T. Nimmo. New York: Oxford University Press, 2019.

OHMLT — *The Oxford Handbook of Martin Luther's Theology*. Ed. Robert Kolb, Irene Dingel, and L'ubomir Batka. New York: Oxford University Press, 2014.

OHRT — *Oxford Handbook of Reformed Theology*. Ed. Michael Allen and Scott R. Swain. New York: Oxford University Press, 2020.

On Providence — Zwingli, Ulrich. *On Providence and Other Essays*. Rpt. Eugene, OR: Wipf & Stock, 1999.

Pastoral — Thurneysen, Eduard. *A Theology of Pastoral Care*. Trans. Jack A. Worthington et al. Richmond, VA: John Knox Press, 1962.

Peacemaking — *Peacemaking: The Believers' Calling*. United Presbyterian Church in the United States of America (1980). Available online at https://www.presbyterianmission.org/resource/peacemaking-believers-calling-text/

Piety — Battles, Ford Lewis. *The Piety of John Calvin: An Anthology Illustrative of the Spirituality of the Reformer*. Grand Rapids, MI: Baker Book House, 1978.

Profound — Van Dyk, Leanne. *A More Profound Alleluia: Theology and Worship in Harmony*. Grand Rapids, MI: William B. Eerdmans, 2005.

R&E — Feldmeth, Nathan P., S. Donald Fortson III, Garth M. Rosell, and Kenneth J. Stewart. *Reformed and Evangelical across Four Centuries: The Presbyterian Story in America*. Grand Rapids, MI: William B. Eerdmans, 2022.

RC   *Reformed Confessions of the Sixteenth Century.* Ed. Arthur C. Cochrane. New Introduction by Jack Rogers. Louisville, KY: Westminster John Knox Press, 2003.

RCS   Reformation Commentary on Scripture. 21 vols. Downer's Grove, IL: InterVarsity Press, n.d.

RD   Bavinck, Herman. *Reformed Dogmatics.* Ed. John Bolt. Trans. John Vriend. 4 vols. Grand Rapids, MI: Baker Academic, 2003–2008.

Restoring   *Restoring Creation for Ecology and Justice.* PC(USA), 1990. Available online at https://www.pcusa.org/resource/search/results/?q=restoring%20creation%20for

Revelation   Forsyth, P. T. *Revelation Old and New: Sermons and Addresses.* Ed. John Huxtable. London: Independent Press, 1962.

School   *The School of Faith: The Catechisms of the Reformed Church.* Trans and ed. Thomas F. Torrance. New York: Harper & Brothers Publishers, 1959.

TOH   Moltmann, Jürgen. *Theology of Hope: On the Ground and the Implications of a Christian Eschatology.* Trans. James W. Leitch. New York: Harper & Row, 1967.

Way   Moltmann, Jürgen. *The Way of Jesus Christ: Christology in Messianic Dimensions.* Trans. Margaret Kohl. San Francisco: HarperSanFrancisco, 1990.

WGT   Barth, Karl. *The Word of God and Theology.* Trans. Amy Marga. London: T&T Clark, 2011.

~

A

Accommodation

A concept (Lat. *accommodatio*) used by John Calvin* and other Reformed theologians, drawn from Latin rhetoricians who adjusted their speeches to the needs and capacities of their hearers, accommodation describes God's* relationship to humans as God adapts and adjusts language to human limitations and understandings.

God's greatness—in transcendence and holiness—means that to be revealed to humans, God must condescend and communicate in ways humans can comprehend and understand, since their capacities are limited by finitude and sin*. Like "nurses commonly do with infants, God is wont in a measure to 'lisp' in speaking to us." God descends "beneath his loftiness" and accommodates the knowledge of God* "to our slight capacity," said Calvin (*Inst.* 1.13.1).

Calvin saw accommodation as God's way with humans. God uses Scripture* to convey the message of salvation*. Scripture is God's revelation*, written by humans. The "mode of accommodation," said Calvin, is for God "to represent himself to us not as he is in himself, but as he seems to us" (*Inst.* 1.17.13). Scripture shows God as Father (Lord's Prayer*), teacher (Law*), and physician (sacraments*) so humans can understand who God is to us.

The supreme example of accommodation is God becoming a human person in Jesus Christ*. In Christ, God "in a manner makes Himself little, in order to accommodate Himself to our comprehension," said Calvin (CNTC 12:250). God uses human language to communicate God's message. In Jesus Christ, God became a human person to reveal God's own self to humans so they could hear and understand God's revelation and the salvation God gives in Jesus Christ.

Adoption

Those who are justified* by faith* in Jesus Christ* and receive salvation* are adopted into the family of God* (the church*) as children of God (John 1:12; Rom. 8:14–17). As such, they "enjoy the liberties and privileges of the children of God" (BC 6.074). This familial relationship through Jesus Christ comes by the power of the Holy Spirit*.

The children of God are released from condemnation under the law* of God and receive the "spirit of adoption" (Rom. 8:15). They are adopted children by God's grace*, whereas Jesus Christ is God's Son by nature (Inst. 2.12.2). The Holy Spirit, who brings faith is the One who enables believers to address God as "Abba! Father!" (Gal. 4:6) and, as John Calvin* said, "to stir us up to call on God with confidence and freedom*" (CNTC 8:167–68). The "spirit of adoption" brings believers assurance—a certainty of salvation. The "spirit of adoption" also brings "the hope* of eternal inheritance of which the Spirit is the earnest and seal, sealed on their hearts" (169; cf. 1 Pet. 1:4). This inheritance for the adopted children of God is "heavenly, and therefore incorruptible and eternal, and such as has been manifested in Christ" (CNTC 8:171). The Spirit is the "pledge of our adoption, so that we are surely convinced of God's Fatherly attitude towards us" (CNTC 11:75). Peter Martyr Vermigli wrote that "nobody can pray in such a way that he calls God his 'Father' unless this had been prompted by the Holy Spirit" (RCS NT VII, 444).

The Spirit in adoption, said Calvin, "raises up our spirits to dare show forth to God their desires" in prayer* (Inst. 3.20.1). Believers will realize the "benefits they receive daily from God's hand are derived from that secret adoption" (3.24.4).

Ascension

The exaltation of Jesus Christ* in his leaving earth and entry into heaven*, forty days after his resurrection* (Acts 1:11; Eph. 4:10). Christ's human nature was changed from a "lower place" to a "higher place." This took place by the power of God* "who raised Christ Jesus from the dead" (Rom. 8:11).

Now Jesus Christ reigns over all without a physical body. Christ's kingdom is inaugurated. Christ's reign over all means "Christ holds in his hands the power of God. He governs in God's name," wrote Karl Barth* (*Faith* 109). So the Apostles' Creed says Christ "sitteth at the right hand of God the Father Almighty." Jesus Christ is Lord of all. All the "powers" of this earth (Col. 1:16; Rom. 8:38) are subservient to the reigning Christ.

Christ's ministries continue in his ascended state. Jesus is the Advocate and Intercessor who speaks on behalf of believers with God (Rom. 8:34; Heb. 7:25; 1 John 2:1–2). John Calvin* wrote that Jesus turns God's eyes "to his own righteousness to avert [God's] gaze from our sins*" (*Inst.* 2.16.16). Jesus "fills with grace* and kindness the throne that for miserable sinners would otherwise have been filled with dread" (2.16.16). Christ's intercession gives "the sure confidence of calling on God" (CNTC 12:56). Christ is for believers so one never prays alone.

Though ascended, Christ is with the church* and believers. For "Christ left us in such a way that his presence might be more useful to us"—since now his presence is not limited to his physical body (*Inst.* 2.16.14). Now Christ is "never absent from us" (Heidelberg Catechism; BC 4.047). Christ is present in life with believers—and in death*.

The charge to the church is: "Seek the things that are above, where Christ is, seated at the right hand of God" (Col. 3:1).

Assurance of Salvation

Can Christian believers have an assurance of salvation? This has been a perplexing question for many Christians through the ages.

Reformed theology* has emphasized that one can be assured of having received the gift of salvation* through faith* in Jesus Christ* by the witness and power of the Holy Spirit*. It is not by human reasoning or human observation that this assurance can come. Assurance of salvation cannot be generated by one's own powers.

Assurance of salvation is a gift of God*. For the Reformed, this assurance is grounded in God's eternal election or predestination*. Being part of the elect, which is the church* of God—God's people united by faith to Jesus Christ—assures one that God's promise to preserve God's people is true (John 10:28) and that those who are justified by faith will be glorified (Rom. 8:29–30). The Spirit of God testifies in one's life that there is "full assurance through Christ" (BC 6.080).

The Westminster Larger Catechism (1648) states: "Such as truly believe in Christ, and endeavor to walk in all good conscience* before him, may, without extraordinary revelation*, by faith grounded upon the truth of God's promises, and by the Spirit enabling them to discern in themselves those graces to which the promises of life are made, and bearing witness with their spirits that they are the children of God, be infallibly assured that they are in the estate of grace, and shall persevere therein unto salvation" (BC 7.190).

Realistically, the Catechism notes that believers may wait long for this assurance and that they may have it "weakened and intermitted, through manifold distempers, sins*, temptations, and desertions; yet are they never left without such a presence and support of the Spirit of God, as keeps them from sinking into utter despair" (BC 7.191).

Atonement

The death* of Jesus Christ* on the cross is the means by which human sin* is forgiven* and reconciliation* with God* takes place. "Atonement" means God and humanity* are "at one." The relationship of love and trust ruptured by human sin is now restored.

Reformed theology* stresses both the work of Christ in his death—what is done ("objective" dimension)—as well as the personal appropriation of Christ's death, where humans confess their sin and by faith* receive the benefits of Christ's death in forgiveness* of their sin ("subjective" dimension). Faith to receive God's loving forgiveness in Christ is the work of the Holy Spirit*.

Reformed theology does not advocate one specific view of how the atonement brings salvation*. Numerous biblical images: sacrifice, atonement, ransom, payment of debts, vicarious satisfaction of a legal penalty, and victory over evil powers have been adopted into "theories of atonement" by theologians. But no one theory "says it all" or can give a full theological explanation. "A Brief Statement of Faith" of the Presbyterian Church (U.S.A.) says simply: "Jesus was crucified, suffering the depths of human pain and giving his life for the sins of the world" (BC 11.2). Karl Barth* wrote that "Jesus Christ is the atonement" (CD IV/1, 34) and "to say atonement is to say Jesus Christ" (CD IV/1, 158).

The enduring power of "Christ crucified" (1 Cor. 1:23) means the atonement reaches out to meet sinners in all their varied conditions and needs. The atonement of the death of Christ brings forgiveness of sin, liberation, freedom* from sin, reconciliation, peace*, and hope* for the defeat of evil and all else that can plague the human heart and mind. All is embraced in the affirmation: "God proves his love for us in that while we still were sinners Christ died for us" (Rom. 5:8).

Authority

Christian faith* as what to believe and how to live is grounded in sources. These provide the criteria by which Christian faith and life are established and evaluated.

The Reformed tradition*, along with Protestantism as a whole, look to Holy Scripture* as God's* revelation* of who God is and what God has done to be the source from which Reformed theology* is derived. Scripture is the written Word of God* and is authoritative because it conveys the word and will of God. For the Reformed, Scripture is the sole authority as the "rule of faith and life," according to the Westminster Confession* (1647; BC 5.010).

Reformed churches have sought to understand Scripture's message for believing and living and have established various creeds and confessions*. These have emerged throughout history* as guides to the theological understandings of Reformed churches. They have "authority" in churches, but it is a "derivative authority": that is, they are authoritative insofar as their teachings are consistent with the teachings of Scripture itself. Reformed theology stands over against Roman Catholic theology, which settles authority in the Roman church's* interpretations of Holy Scripture along with its own church traditions. For the Reformed, the Scriptures "have sufficient authority of themselves," as the Second Helvetic Confession (1566) says (BC 5.001).

Reason*, another potential source of authority, is recognized by the Reformed as being affected by sin* and thus cannot be a source of the knowledge of God* or of salvation*. Only as reason is led by God's Holy Spirit* to understand God's revelation in Scripture can it function as a means of authority.

The Anabaptist tradition has focused authority in Christian experience. The Methodist tradition has approached authority through a quadrilateral: Scripture, tradition, reason, and experience. The Reformed rejected the "inner light" (Quakerism) or a role for experience as authoritative, apart from God's revelation in Scripture. Genuine Christian experience always accords with God's Word in Scripture.

B

Baptism

Baptism, with the Lord's Supper*, is one of two sacraments* of Reformed churches. In baptism, "we are engrafted into Christ Jesus, to be made partakers of his righteousness, by which our sins* are covered and remitted," says the Scots Confession (1560; BC 3.21). Baptism is a sign of God's* covenant* and those baptized become part of the people of God, the church*. Baptism is "a sign of initiation for God's people, since by it the elect of God are consecrated to God" for the Second Helvetic Confession (1566; BC 5.185).

Baptism is administered once to those who profess faith* in Jesus Christ*, in the name of the triune God. For "baptism once received continues for all of life, and is a perpetual sealing of our adoption*" (BC 5.186). The further theological dimensions of baptism include "the solemn admission of the party baptized into the visible Church, but also to be unto him a sign and seal of the covenant* of grace*, of his ingrafting into Christ, of regeneration*, of remission of sins, and of his giving up unto God, through Jesus Christ, to walk in newness of life" (6.154).

Reformed theology* advocates infant baptism since "infants as well as adults are included in God's covenant and people, and they, no less than adults, are promised deliverance from sin through Christ's blood and the Holy Spirit* who produces faith. Therefore, by baptism, the sign of the covenant, they too should be incorporated into the Christian church and distinguished from the children of unbelievers. This was done in the Old Testament* by circumcision, which was replaced in the New Testament* by baptism," according to the Heidelberg Catechism (1563; BC 4.074). Here, Reformed churches are distinct from Anabaptist churches, which practice only adult or "believer's" baptism. For the Reformed, the rite of Confirmation is established for those baptized as infants to confess their faith as adults.

Barmen, Theological Declaration of

The Theological Declaration of Barmen (1934) was a statement of the Confessing Synod of the German Evangelical Church in the face of the German political situation. The Declaration was primarily written by Karl Barth*. It was a theological appraisal opposing "German Christians" who supported the ideology of Adolf Hitler and National Socialism. Hitler sought to take over the German church*. From this Declaration, the Confessing Church of Germany arose. The Declaration provided a theological basis for the church's struggles throughout World War II.

The Declaration propounded six theses, each quoting Scripture*, which spoke to the German context. Accompanying each thesis was a denial: "We reject the false doctrine*. . . ." Key is the first thesis: "Jesus Christ*, as he is attested for us in Holy Scripture, is the one Word of God* which we have to hear and which we have to trust and obey in life and death*." This was followed by the denial: "We reject the false doctrine, as though the church could and would have to acknowledge as a source of its proclamation, apart from and besides this one Word of God, still other events and powers, figures and truths, as God's* revelation*" (BC 8.11, 12).

The Declaration proclaims Jesus Christ as "God's assurance of the forgiveness* of all our sins*" and as "God's mighty claim upon our whole life" (BC 8.14); the church belongs solely to Christ (8.17); church offices are not for dominion but for "the exercise of the ministry*" (8.20); the state is appointed by God for the task of "providing for justice* and peace*" (8.22); and the church's commission is to deliver "the message of the free grace* of God to all people in Christ's stead" (8.26).

The Declaration continues to affect church confessions*, emphasizing the need to confess faith* in Jesus Christ.

Barth, Karl

Karl Barth (1886–1968) was one of the most influential and significant Reformed theologians of the twentieth century.

Barth was born in Basel, Switzerland, and studied theology under liberal theologians, including Adolf von Harnack. He was a pastor (1911–1921) and spoke against his former teachers when they supported World War I. His *Commentary on Romans* (1919; rev. 1922) presented a theological interpretation of this letter. Barth was called to teach at Göttingen, Germany, and with Eduard Thurneysen, Emil Brunner, and others began to develop "dialectical theology" (also: "theology of the Word of God*," "theology of crisis," and later, "Neo-Orthodoxy*"). Barth and colleagues sought a new basis for theology and talk of God* in the Word of God—known in Jesus Christ* as witnessed to in Holy Scripture*.

In 1935, Barth began to teach at Basel, where he stayed the rest of his life. He opposed Hitler through the Confessing Church and was the primary author of the Theological Declaration of Barmen*.

Barth's multivolume *Church Dogmatics* (1936–1977) was unfinished but was thoroughly Christological* in centering dogmatics in Jesus Christ as "the Word made flesh" (John 1:14). Throughout, Barth reenvisioned Reformed doctrines* including creation*, providence*, sin*, covenant*, and election* to accord with the free God of grace* in sending Jesus Christ to die and be raised again for the sin of the whole world. Sinners receive justification* in Christ through faith* and reconciliation* with God their Creator. In sanctification*, those who believe live out their salvation* in Jesus Christ in the context of the Christian community, the church*, where it must be lived. Barth also said the vocation* of humanity* is to witness to God's reconciliation. Salvation is the work of the Holy Spirit*. The difference between Christians and others is that Christians know salvation in Christ. Their task is to witness to it to others.

Barth's influence continues today in various ways. Cornelis Van der Kooi notes that many of Barth's "basic decisions," as well as "the overall framework in which he worked, have slowly gained traction in the broader world of Reformed theology*" (*OHKB* 655). Among theologians influenced by Barth are Robert W. Jenson, Kathryn Tanner, Daniel L. Migliore, John Webster, and Stanley Hauerwas.

Belhar, Confession of

The Confession of Belhar was written in South Africa in 1982. It was adopted as a church* confession by the Dutch Reformed Mission Church (DRMC) in 1986. The Confession was a strong theological statement in the context of the practice of apartheid (racial separation) in South Africa. It emphasized that Christians are one in Jesus Christ* and that the church is called to live out God's* intention for all humanity*. Uniquely, the Confession of Belhar emerged from the DRMC, a mission church that had been founded to serve the "colored" population in 1881, which issued a critique of the Dutch Reformed Church, its founding church communion.

The Confession has five sections. It features a Trinitarian opening that states the relationship of the Trinity* to the church (BC 10.1). Three sections follow and present the themes of unity (10.3), reconciliation* (10.5), and justice* (10.7). It concludes by affirming that Jesus Christ is Lord and with a trinitarian benediction (10.9).

Belhar confesses belief "that Christ's work of reconciliation is made manifest in the church as the community of believers who have been reconciled with God and with one another" and that this unity is both "a gift and an obligation for the church of Jesus Christ" (BC 10.3). This means a rejection of any doctrine* that "absolutizes either natural diversity or the sinful separation of people" (10.4). An implication of the belief in justice, says the Confession, is that "in following Christ the church must witness against all the powerful and privileged who selfishly seek their own interests and thus control and harm others" (10.7).

Belhar's strong voice on church unity, reconciliation, and justice has encouraged other global churches to pursue these Christian essentials while they struggle against oppression and pursue justice. Churches recognize the theological foundations of their efforts for political goals that reflect the integrity of the Gospel of Jesus Christ.

Bucer, Martin

Martin Bucer (1491–1551) was an important Reformed theologian who influenced John Calvin* and helped in shaping Reformed theology*. Bucer was vigorous in trying to bring reconciliation with Lutherans, a reflection of his ecumenical outlook. He was an important influence on the Tetrapolitan Confession (1530) and, with Philip Melanchthon, led Protestant–Roman Catholic colloquies, or formal conversations (1539–1541).

Bucer was born in Sélestat, Alsace, and became a Dominican. He was influenced by Erasmus and became a supporter of church* reform through the works of Martin Luther. After leaving the Dominican order, he married and moved to Strassbourg. There he became a leader of the Protestant Reformation in the city.

Through his leadership, the city became known for toleration. Bucer stressed church discipline* along with church doctrine* and polity*. Calvin spent three years in Strassbourg (1539–1541), where he imbibed Bucer's thought in biblical commentaries on the issues of predestination* and the Lord's Supper* and especially worship* and church polity. This included the offices of elder* and deacon*. Calvin enacted Bucer's vision of a reformed church and society in Geneva throughout his ministry* there.

The Augsburg Interim (1548) forced Bucer's exile from Strassbourg. Thomas Cranmer invited him to England where he became Regius Professor of Divinity at the University of Cambridge (1549). Here he influenced the Anglican Church, especially in its *Book of Common Prayer* (1552). Bucer's vision of a nation featuring a reformed church was laid out in his *The Kingdom of Christ* (1557), which was presented to King Edward VI.

Bucer's strong sense of the Christian community in communion with Jesus Christ* led him to emphasize the church as a community of love. Bucer saw "love of one's neighbour as the definition of faith*" (*Common Places* 195–96). This meant the church should be active in poor relief and providing for human need.

Bullinger, Heinrich

Heinrich Bullinger (1504–1575) was a Swiss-German reformer who succeeded Huldrych Zwingli*, after his battlefield death* in 1531, as the main pastor of the Zurich church*. Bullinger was a prolific writer, producing a variety of theological works. He preached approximately seventy-five hundred sermons, with around six hundred being published. Bullinger's *Decades* (1549), featuring fifty sermons, was his most well-known work. Some twelve thousand of his manuscript letters also exist.

While a student at Cologne, Bullinger was deeply influenced by works by Erasmus, Martin Luther, and Philip Melanchthon. In 1523, he supported Zwingli's reform in Zurich and participated in the Berne Disputation (1528). Bullinger came to Zurich and became Zwingli's successor. In 1549, he and John Calvin* authored the *Consensus Tigurinus* (Agreement of Zurich).

Bullinger was the primary author of the Second Helvetic Confession (1566), which became an important Reformed confession. His theological writings are marked by an ongoing pastoral concern. He stressed especially the doctrines of the covenant*, election*, Christology*, and saw the center of the faith* as God's* free grace* in Jesus Christ*, made known to us through Scripture* and received by faith.

The church was central for Bullinger. He believed Christ came and died to "make one church and fellowship" (*Decades* 3:259). The church is "the company, communion, congregation, multitude, or fellowship of all that profess the name of Christ" (*Decades* 1:161). The fellowship of the church is of those saints who are united with Christ and with each other in Christ.

Bullinger forged his own views of the Lord's Supper*, distinguishing them from the Lutheran and Roman Catholic teachings. His views of the Supper and on predestination* were slightly different than Calvin's and testify to the diversities within Reformed theology* in its formative years. Bullinger emphasized the Christian life and wrote that "the preaching* of the Word of God* is the Word of God" (BC 5.004).

C

Calvin, John

John Calvin (1509–1564) was a highly influential French Protestant reformer who served as a theologian and pastor in Geneva. Calvin imbibed Humanist perspectives from his teachers and published a commentary on Seneca's *De Clementia* (1531). At some point, he experienced a "sudden conversion*" and became active among French Protestants in Paris. In 1533, Calvin was forced to flee and traveled through Europe, publishing his first theological work, *Psychopannychia* (1534), against the notion of "soul sleep." The first edition of his *Institutes of the Christian Religion* was published in 1536.

In August 1536, Calvin arrived in Geneva and was enjoined by William Farel to stay and help with church* reform. After controversy, Calvin left for Strassbourg, where he worked with the leading pastor, Martin Bucer*. A new edition of the *Institutes* was published in 1539, and Calvin was asked to return to Geneva in 1541. Calvin led the city in reforms until his death*. He preached, led the pastors, and wrote biblical commentaries and theological treatises. His *Institutes* appeared in Latin and French versions, the last (Latin) published in 1559. It became a standard text in Reformed theology*.

Calvin's theology emphasized God's* gracious initiative in providing salvation* in Jesus Christ*. The "elect" of God are those to whom the Holy Spirit* grants the gift of faith* in Christ as the means to the forgiveness* of sin* and new life lived in union with Christ. The church is the "communion of saints*" who live as Christ's disciples through the power of the Holy Spirit in sanctification*—growing in holiness, love, and service to God and others. God's providence* leads the church and believers through the "zigs and zags" of life. Ultimately, "God will be King in the world when all submit to his will" (*Inst.* 3.20.43) in the coming Kingdom of God*.

Calvinism

The development of the theology of John Calvin* emerged into more systematic forms from the seventeenth century onward. Aspects of Calvin's thought were given more detailed formulations amid the new questions and conflicts that arose in later periods. Calvinism is one term used to describe the theological works of Reformed theologians who built on Calvin's insights and established those theological understandings in a more structured, codified form. These developments have also been called Reformed Orthodoxy*. Varieties of Reformed theologies developed among a number of theologians. Scholars have debated ways in which the later Reformed theologians developed Calvin's views and whether they were salutary developments or not. The specific contexts of the later theologians need always be recognized.

Calvinism, in its various historical forms, "emerged in marginal cities in central Europe, gradually establishing a presence throughout Europe and eventually around the world" (*Calvinism*, xii). Areas of particular strength for Calvinism were the Netherlands and the British Isles. Puritans in Holland and England as well as the Scotch-Irish came to America and were influential in establishing a theology and a cultural system of Calvinism in the developing American nation. Emerging democratic institutions in the United States were influenced by Calvinism through emphases on education and industry. Calvinism was a contributing factor of some measure for capitalism and the Protestant work* ethic. Calvinist church* polities, which established shared church leadership with clergy/laity cooperation, provided models for other societal institutions.

Calvinism around the globe—while emphasizing corporateness and fueled by biblical and theological mandates toward social service, justice*, and peace*—has also been subject to church splits based on theological differences within a wider Reformed/Calvinist family of believers.

Yet Calvinism spread around the globe through "the ordinary—and often accidental—efforts of average pastors and lay people" (*Calvinism* xii).

Catechism

From the Greek *katechein* ("to instruct"; "to teach"), a catechism is a means of instruction, often in a question-answer form. Christian churches have used catechisms to convey basic Christian beliefs, often with the aim of preparing individuals for church* membership.

Numerous catechisms were prepared in the Reformation period, many for use in Reformed churches, to instruct persons—often children—in Christian doctrine*. The rite of Confirmation was a time for children to confess their personal faith*.

Among important Reformed catechisms have been John Calvin's* Geneva Catechism (1538; 1541), the Heidelberg Catechism (1563), Craig's Catechism (1581), and the Westminster Larger and Shorter Catechism (1648), which reflect teachings of the Westminster Confession of Faith* (1647; see *School*).

Classic questions and answers of Reformed catechisms include the Heidelberg Catechism, Q.1: "What is your only comfort in life and in death*?" A. "That I am not my own, but belong—body and soul, in life and in death—to my faithful Savior, Jesus Christ*" (BC 4.001). The Westminster Shorter Catechism, Q.1 asks, "What is the chief end of man?" and answers, "Man's chief end is to glorify God*, and to enjoy him forever" (BC 7.001).

In 2006, the Presbyterian Church in Canada produced *A Catechism for Today*. In 1998, the Presbyterian Church (USA) approved three new catechisms: *Belonging to God: A First Catechism*, for children, and *The Study Catechism*, which appeared in Confirmation and Full versions. An introduction to the *Book of Catechisms* (2001) indicates that catechisms embody "the *church's* teachings rather than the insights or opinions of individuals." They are important in the church's life to enhance its "continuous conversation about the meaning of Christian faith as well as in its task of handing the faith on from one generation to the next" (BC vii). Catechisms also "provide persons with a foundation that enables them to exercise freedom* of conscience* within Christian faith" (vii).

Christology

Study of the person and work of Jesus Christ has led Christian theology and churches to come to theological convictions about who Jesus was and what Jesus did.

Reformed theology* has accepted the consensus of the early church*, expressed in credal statements that reflect scriptural teachings. Key is the confession of the true humanity and full divinity of Jesus Christ as the eternal Son of God*. Jesus Christ became human to reconcile* humanity* through his death* on the cross through forgiveness* from the power of sin*. In his resurrection* and ascension*, the risen Christ defeated the power of sin and provides the way to salvation* and eternal life through the power of the Holy Spirit* to those who believe in him by faith*.

Christologically, Reformed theology has rejected ubiquity*, as taught in Lutheranism. It denies the view that the risen Christ is everywhere bodily present (Heidelberg Catechism, qq. 47–48). Reformed theology has taught that after his incarnation*, Christ is present and active beyond the flesh united to himself. This is called the *extra-Calvinisticum**. John Calvin* emphasized the "threefold office" of Christ (*munus triplex**)—Prophet, Priest, and King—as a way of uniting the person of Christ with the work of Christ (*Inst.* 2.15).

Traditionally, Reformed theologians have begun Christology "from above," stressing the divinity of Christ: "The Word became flesh and lived among us" (John 1:14). Karl Barth* began that way but later emphasized "the humanity of God" in Jesus Christ—a Christology "from below." A major contribution of Jürgen Moltmann* is his emphasis on "the crucified God," which sees "the death of Jesus on the cross" as "the *centre* of all Christian theology" with "all Christian statements about God, about creation*, about sin and death" having "their focal point in the crucified Christ" (*Crucified* 204).

Church

Reformed theology* affirms the Nicene Creed's confession of the "one holy catholic and apostolic Church" (BC 1.3).

These "marks of the church" are expressions of the Reformed theological conviction from the Westminster Confession* (1647) that the church "consists of the whole number of the elect, that have been, are, or shall be gathered into one, under Christ, the head thereof" (BC 6.140). The church as the "communion of saints*" is "invisible" in that those who are its members—by faith* in Jesus Christ*—are known only to God*. The church is "visible" in that the church exists on earth as those who confess Jesus Christ as their Lord and Savior. The church is marked by its institutional "visibility" as those who worship* and serve God in Jesus Christ.

The church is "one" under the Lordship of Christ. The church is "holy" not based in its own virtues or goodness, but in being "set apart" for God's purposes and living in "union with Christ*," who gives to the church the righteousness and holiness it cannot attain for itself. The church is "catholic" in that it extends throughout the earth. The church is "apostolic" in that it continues to preach and teach the Scriptures* as the source of its witness to who Jesus Christ is and what Christ has done.

The church is a theological community. It is God's gracious accommodation* to sinful humanity* by providing salvation* in Christ and gathering those who believe into one body through which they can together serve Jesus Christ and the world for which Christ died. Karl Barth* called the church "the earthly-historical form of existence of Jesus Christ Himself" (CD IV/1, 661). The church gathers in worship to render praise and thanks to God and to "be sent into the world" as God's "reconciling community" through the power of the Holy Spirit* (BC 9.31).

Communion of Saints

This phrase from the Apostles' Creed (Lat. *sanctorum communio*) has been variously interpreted. Middle Ages understandings related it to the sacraments*. A second view is confessing faith* in the church* here and now—the "saints of God*" gathered together in "union" and mutual love in the visible church.

A strong Reformed emphasis has been to see the phrase referring to all the people of God—past, present, and future: All those who, through God's election*, have constituted the "invisible" church through all ages form a "communion of saints" that embraces all those in the "society of Christ" (*Inst.* 4.1.3) in all times. "Whatever benefits God confers upon them, they should in turn share with one another," wrote John Calvin*. This is a comprehensive view of the church.

The Heidelberg Catechism (1563) notes that all believers in the communion of saints, this "community," share "in Christ and in all his treasures and gifts" (BC 4.055). All the benefits of Christian life and existence come to the church—and its members—from Jesus Christ*. The church lives from its Lord, who shares his benefits with all who are elect in him (Eph. 1:4).

The Catechism goes on to say, "Each member should consider it a duty to use these gifts readily and joyfully for the service and enrichment of the other members" (BC 4.055). The church is to share gifts given, in joyfulness, in service to others. This binds the church together in common purpose and in service to "the head of the church," Jesus Christ (Eph. 5:23), for "anyone united to the Lord becomes one spirit with him" (1 Cor. 6:17). This union—and communion—of believers with Jesus Christ is the relationship each has with another in the church. All is grounded in the electing call of God, which forms a people of God throughout history*.

Conscience

What is right or wrong in the eyes of God* is an important topic. "Conscience" has been a much-considered issue, with mentions of "conscience" in Scripture* (Rom. 2:15; 1 Cor. 4:4).

John Calvin* spoke of conscience as "a sense of divine judgment*" within persons, a "certain mean between God and man" that "does not allow man to suppress within himself what he knows, but pursues him to the point of convicting him" (*Inst.* 3.19.15).

Yet a "good conscience" is also possible before God (1 Pet. 3:21) where "peace of mind" can come when one is "convinced of Christ's grace*." This enables us "fearlessly to present ourselves before God" (see Heb. 10:2). By grace, "sin* may no longer accuse us" (*Inst.* 3.19.15).

Guidance for how one should live in making decisions—so conscience becomes either friend or foe—was given by Puritan Reformed theologians such as William Perkins and William Ames, who prepared books on "cases of conscience" to bring the resources of faith* to bear on ethical issues. The goal for one, said Ames, was to develop "a practical judgment" applied to good or evil so it "becomes a rule to direct his will" (*De conscientia* [1630] I, i, 3, in *Marrow*). For Ames, those who live in "newness of life"—as Christians, in Jesus Christ* (Rom. 6:3, 4)—possess an enlightened conscience so conscience is a person's "judgment of himself according to God's judgment of him" (*De conscientia* I, i, preamble, in *Marrow*). Humans living according to God is the crux of conscience for Ames. The basic function of conscience in Christian faith is "to examine the relationship between man and God and therein to find answers to genuine questions and to produce grounds for decision and action" (*Marrow* 42–43).

Conversion

Biblically, "conversion" is a turning into a new direction in one's life. Saul of Tarsus was a persecutor of Christians. After encountering the living Christ (Acts 9), he became "Paul," and "began to proclaim Jesus in the synagogues, saying, 'He is the Son of God*'" (Acts 9:20).

Theologically, conversion marks a life-changing transformation in an encounter with God's gracious love and forgiveness* of sin*. The "experience" of conversion varies, and no one experience is normative. Key is the appropriation of God's grace* in Jesus Christ* by faith*, forgiveness of sin, and repentance*, which in turn marks this change of life into a life of love and obedience to God and service to others as a disciple of Jesus Christ. "New life" comes by the power of the Holy Spirit*.

Reformed theology* ascribes the full work of conversion to God's will and electing power. Theological controversies between Reformed and other theologies—such as Arminianism—have led to different understandings of conversion in different theological groups. God's initiation of salvation* (conversion) is basic for the Reformed, as are the theological actions of regeneration* and justification*.

The Reformed emphasize humans have no "free will*" to be able to "choose" to believe in Jesus Christ. The pervasive power of sin means that by themselves, humans will always choose sinful actions or directions. No human power can lead to one believing in God's grace in Jesus Christ. Humans can believe only by the work of the Holy Spirit, who brings faith in Jesus Christ.

Further debates have centered on whether conversion is a "single act" or a "gradual process" and whether or not one must be able to point to a definite time or place where one was "converted." Reformed theology teaches conversion in some form occurs for all Christians, while recognizing that each conversion is unique.

Covenant

Covenant is a rich theological term in Reformed theology*. Throughout Scripture*, God* makes covenants with persons—such as Noah (Gen. 9:1–17), Abraham (Gen. 15), and the people of Israel (Exod. 19) in the Old Testament*, and, supremely, in Jesus Christ* (1 Cor. 11:23–26) in the New Testament*. These covenants indicate the relationship between God and humanity* as God promises blessings upon communities of people.

Sixteenth-century Reformed theologians developed "covenant" as a significant theological doctrine*. Heinrich Bullinger* and Huldrych Zwingli* emphasized covenant in biblical thought as they reacted to Anabaptism. John Calvin* frequently mentioned God's covenant and its meanings.

Reformed theology was often called "Covenant theology" in the seventeenth-century. Theologians such as Johannes Cocceius and Hermann Witsius developed major theological works focused on God's relationship with humanity expressed in covenants. The Westminster Confession* (1647) taught that in God's "covenant of grace*," God "freely offered unto sinners life and salvation* by Jesus Christ, requiring of them faith* in him, that they may be saved" (BC 6.039). Further, "sacraments* are holy signs and seals of the covenant of grace" (6.149). These theological works also said God had initially established a "covenant of works" in which humanity was promised eternal life* on the condition that Adam was obedient to the Word of God*. Some believed this view lacked biblical support in relation to a promise of eternal life.

Reformed theology stresses the unity of the Old and New Testaments*. From the covenant with Abraham through God's interactions with Israel in the giving of the Law* of God to the promise to Jeremiah (Jer. 31:31–34) of a "new covenant," Jesus Christ is seen as the culmination and fulfillment of God's covenants. God's relationship with humans is completed in the work of Jesus Christ. The church* is a covenant community, drawing its life from its Lord, Jesus Christ.

Creation

The Westminster Confession* (1647) conveys important dimensions of Reformed theology's* views about creation: "It pleased God* the Father, Son, and Holy Ghost, for the manifestation of the glory of his eternal power, wisdom, and goodness, in the beginning, to create or make of nothing the world, and all things therein, whether visible or invisible, in the space of six days, and all very good" (BC 6.022).

While the "six days" mentioned is no longer taken literally, the theological declarations of the Confession continue to have lasting impact for Reformed theology. Other Reformed confessional statements also express Westminster's emphases. The "Confession of 1967" says: "In its beauty and vastness, sublimity and awfulness, order and disorder, the world reflects to the eye of faith* the majesty and mystery of its Creator" (BC 9.16).

Creation is the work of the triune God—the three persons of the Trinity*. Creation expresses the glory of God (Ps. 19:1), and when God is known for who God truly is, creation is a "natural revelation*" as the glory of God is perceived by Christian believers in the created order. John Calvin* said, "Wherever we cast our eyes, all things they meet are works of God" (Inst. 1.14.20). He referred to creation as a "dazzling theater" (1.5.8).

Reformed theology stresses the relationship between God's creation and God's providence*. The Second Helvetic Confession (1566) discusses God's providence in governing "all things," before discussing God's "creation of all things" (BC 5.029, 5.032). God is involved in creation, unlike later Deism, which taught that God does not intervene in creation at all.

Since God is Creator, humans, who are created in the "image of God*" (Gen. 1:27), belong to God and are to serve God. Inquiring into the nature and workings of God's creation is an ongoing human activity, supported by Reformed theological understandings.

Creeds and Confessions

Reformed theology* has paid great attention to the creeds and confessions of Reformed churches. Creeds are compact expressions of theological beliefs. Confessions of faith* are longer, public declarations and official statements of what a community of Christians believes. A distinctive mark of Reformed churches since the sixteenth century is that Reformed churches in new areas or new Reformed bodies of Christians confess their faith and often write a confessional statement. These affirmations of the church's* faith always relate to God*, to the church itself, and to the world. They are statements of theological and missional identity. The Reformed theological tradition* has been prolific in producing confessional documents as expressions also of Reformed theology.

Reformed confessions—as Reformed theology itself—see all confessional documents as subordinate to Scripture*. Creeds and confessions express understandings of what the Scriptures teach. The Presbyterian Church (USA) has noted that confessions have a "provisional authority*"—they are subject to revision and correction since they are written by limited, fallible, and sinful persons and churches. They have a "temporary authority" because faith means always being open to hear a new and fresh word of God* through the Holy Spirit*. Confessions have a "relative authority" since they are always subject to the higher authority of the Scriptures, which guide us into understanding God's will and work. (See "The Confessional Nature of the Church" in BC 442).

Important Reformed confessions of the sixteenth century include the First and Second Helvetic Confessions (1536; 1566), the Belgic Confession (1561), and the Scots Confession (1560), among many others. Today, new confessions have been written in Africa and Asia, including the Confession of Faith of the United Church of Christ of Japan (1954), the Confession of Belhar* (1982) in South Africa, and the Confession of Faith of the Presbyterian Church of Taiwan (1979).

D

Deacons

Reformed theology* as expressed in Reformed churches recognize deacon (Gr. *diakonos*: "servant"; Lat. *minister*) as an ordained office in the church*, to be held by laity. Reformed polity* has recognized "elder" and "deacon" as distinct offices, though in some churches, the work* of deacons has been subsumed in the office of elder.

New Testament* precedents show the work of deacons to be meeting the needs of the poor and needy through benevolence and personal care (Acts 6:1–6; 1 Tim. 3:8–13; 5:9–10; Rom. 12:8; 16:1–2). John Calvin* saw the importance of this office as service and love of neighbor (*Inst.* 4.4.5). This office, according to Calvin, is a permanent necessity for the church to be rightly ordered.

Deacons are to give institutional expression to love of neighbor by using resources to help those in need and thus to love and serve as Jesus commanded (John 15:12; Luke 22:27). This magnifies the effect of personal benevolence and care—to which all Christians are called. Boards of deacons, under the authority* of the session (elders* and pastor) in some churches, are main voices for social witness and issues of justice* and peace*. Care and love for neighbor is seen to be more all-embracing than only traditional activities of meeting individual needs. In Reformed churches, the office of deacon has been open both to men and women.

One Presbyterian denomination says, "The ministry* of deacon as set forth in Scripture* is one of compassion, witness, and service, sharing in the redeeming love of Jesus Christ* for the poor, the hungry, the sick, the lost, the friendless, the oppressed, those burdened by unjust policies or structures, or anyone in distress. Persons of spiritual character, honest repute, exemplary lives, brotherly and sisterly love, sincere compassion, and sound judgment should be chosen for this ministry" (BO G-2.0201).

Death

When physical life ceases, death occurs. Sin*, according to Reformed theology*, brought death to the created order (Rom. 6:23). The consequence of sin is spiritual death, which extends to all who sin (Rom. 5:12).

Yet the finality of death is not the last word in life. Reformed theology emphasizes that deliverance from death is possible through the power of the death and resurrection* of Jesus Christ*. Christ's resurrection shows God's* power over death so that those who are "in Christ" by faith* receive "the free gift of God is eternal life in Christ Jesus our Lord" (Rom. 6:23). The Heidelberg Catechism (1653) says that "by his resurrection he has overcome death, so that he might make us share in the righteousness he obtained for us by his death" (BC 4.045).

Physical death is not the end of human existence. The final word is the triumph of Jesus Christ which brings the hope of eternal life. The Second Helvetic Confession (1566) notes that "our Lord reconciled all the faithful to the heavenly Father, made expiation for sins, disarmed death, overcame damnation and hell*, and by his resurrection from the dead brought again and restored life and immortality" (BC 5.076).

The victory of Christ over death and the gift of eternal life* given to believers is the scriptural word of hope* and assurance. As Herman Bavinck put it, "Scripture* is not the book of death, but of life, of everlasting life through Jesus Christ our Lord. It tells us, in oft-repeated and unmistakable terms, of the dreaded reality of death, but it proclaims to us still more loudly the wonderful power of the life which is in Christ Jesus" (ISBE 2:813).

Believers in Jesus Christ are deeply comforted in the faith that "in life and in death we belong to God" (BC 11.1).

Decrees of God

Reformed theologians in the post-Reformation period spoke of the decree(s) of God to name all things God* wills and orders (Eph. 1:11). More specifically, the term referred to God's eternal predestination*. The divine decrees are what God actually wills and are prior to all things, expressing God's divine essence. The divine will does not change over time. The Westminster Confession* (1647) states, "God from all eternity did by the most wise and holy counsel of his own will, freely and unchangeably ordain whatsoever comes to pass" (BC 6.014).

The Confession goes on to indicate that the divine decrees do not make God "the author of sin*; nor is violence offered to the will of the creatures, nor is the liberty or contingency of second causes taken away, but rather established" (BC 6.014). While God's eternal decree to "act" is the "primary cause" of all things, humanity's* acts and activities are "second" or "secondary" causes. Thus, human responsibility is real, even as God's eternal will is expressed and enacted. These views are part of a theological tradition* of controversy over the relation of human acts to the acts of God, notably in controversies between Augustine and Pelagius and the Reformed and Arminian traditions.

The decrees relate specifically to salvation* and God's eternal decision to elect individuals to receive the gift of salvation through faith* by the work of the Holy Spirit* in time. The question of what the divine decree means for those "nonelect" has been contested in Reformed thought.

Varieties of ways of understanding these issues have emerged in Reformed theology*, from John Calvin* through Heinrich Bullinger* and Ursinus to later theologians: Friedrich Daniel Ernst Schleiermacher* and Karl Barth*. Barth recast election*, specifically advocating for a strong Christocentric emphasis: Jesus Christ* is both the "object" and "subject" of election. God "chose us in Christ" (Eph. 1:4).

Descent into Hell

The Apostles' Creed affirms that Jesus "descended into hell*" (Lat. *descensus ad inferos*) after his death* and burial and before he rose from the dead on "the third day." In some sense, Jesus is said to have descended to "the realm of the dead" (OT: Hades, Sheol) before his resurrection* (1 Pet. 3:19).

Reformed theology* has seen Christ's "descent into hell" as the final stage of Christ's humiliation, his earthly life. Lutheran theologians have viewed it as the first stage of Christ's exaltation, his victorious work of glorification.

Some Reformed—Martin Bucer* and Theodore Beza—viewed Christ's descent as identical with his burial. Ames said Christ's three days is "described as existence in Hell" (*Marrow* 144). John Calvin* related Christ's "descent" to the suffering of Christ's soul since he had to "undergo the severity of God's* vengeance, to appease his wrath and satisfy his just judgment*" (*Inst.* 2.16.10; Isa. 53:5). This was the spiritual torment Christ endured: "He paid a greater and more excellent price in suffering in his soul the terrible torments of a condemned and forsaken man" (*Inst.* 2.16.10). Calvin spoke of Christ's "wrestling hand to hand with the devil's power, with the dread of death, with the pains of hell" and that "he was victorious and triumphed over them, that in death we may not now fear those things which our Prince has swallowed up" (1 Pet. 3:22; *Inst.* 2.16.11).

The Heidelberg Catechism (1563) adopted an application of this view for Christian believers. To the Question, "Why does the creed add, 'He descended to hell'?" the Answer is, "To assure me during attacks of deepest dread and temptation that Christ my Lord by suffering unspeakable anguish, pain, and terror of soul on the cross but also earlier, has delivered me from hellish anguish and torment'" (Isa. 53:10; Matt. 27:46; BC 4.044).

Discipline, Church

The Scots Confession (1560) indicates three marks of the church*: They are "the true preaching* of the Word of God*," the "right administration of the sacraments* of Christ Jesus," and third, "ecclesiastical discipline uprightly ministered, as God's* Word prescribes, whereby vice is repressed, and virtue nourished" (BC 3.18). In this, the Scottish church followed the Confession of Faith of the English-Speaking Congregation in Geneva (1556; RC 135). This went beyond John Calvin*, who saw the "Word of God purely preached and heard" and the sacraments "administered according to Christ's institution" as the two marks of where "a church of God exists" (Inst. 4.1.9; Bucer and the Belgic Confession [art. 29; RC 210] have three marks).

The ways in which spiritual oversight of churches and their members took shape in the variety of places where Reformed churches ministered, varied. In Zurich, Huldrych Zwingli* and Heinrich Bullinger* put church discipline in the purview of the civil government*. Church and society were blended. For Martin Bucer* and Calvin, church discipline—including excommunication—should take place through courts of the church. Churches were ruled by elders* (Presbyterian polity*) and were separate from civil government. In 1562, French Reformed churches developed a congregational form where the local congregation imposed church discipline. In the American colonies, New England Congregationalism was prominent, with Presbyterian polity also becoming important.

At its best, church discipline is to have a spiritual and pastoral basis and seek outcomes which are redemptive and as restorative as possible. The Book of Order of the Presbyterian Church (USA) says, "The church administers discipline as an expression of the authority* of Christ, for the sake of the welfare of the church, and toward the goal of redemption and reconciliation, by God's grace*'" (BO W-4.0504). This goal is shared by other Reformed bodies.

Doctrine

Doctrine (Lat. *doctrina*, "teaching") is used in several senses. "Christian doctrine" refers to the teachings Christian churches have developed through the centuries. Various church* or denominational traditions* may speak of specific understandings that mark their traditions, such as "Reformed doctrine," as ways people in Reformed churches understand specifics of Christian doctrine. More particularly, the term can be used to refer to a specific doctrine such as the doctrine of faith* or predestination*.

Reformed theology* emerges from the theological writings of Protestant theologians such as Huldrych Zwingli*, John Calvin*, Francis Turretin, and others who formulated understandings of the doctrines of the church, giving them specific focuses and emphases. Their "doctrines" or "theology," as a whole, stood in contrast, at points, with other "theologies" of the Reformation era found in the Lutheran and Anabaptist traditions.

Reformed doctrine, as Reformed theology itself, seeks to be faithful and consistent expressions of the teachings of Scripture*. The Bible, as the Word of God* written—God's* special revelation*—is the source for theological and doctrinal authority*. Doctrines are expressions of Scripture's organized teachings for the sake of the church. Confessionals statements, in ecclesiastical traditions, convey what their authors—and churches—believe about the *loci* ("places") or themes/doctrines of Scripture.

Doctrines, as human expressions of biblical teachings, are revisable. They are always subject to further interpretations, or modifications, based on new insights or understandings, particularly of biblical texts. Confessional documents of churches are historic expressions of what the church believed at that point in history*.

Likewise, Reformed theology has origins and historical developments, as well as expressions by a number of Reformed theologians. Major figures in Reformed theology from Calvin to Turretin to Friedrich Daniel Ernst Schleiermacher* to Karl Barth* to Jürgen Moltmann* have developed their theologies, each approaching doctrinal topics in their own manners. Yet all also believed their theological work was grounded in Scripture.

E

Economics

The production of goods and services throughout a political entity (such as a country) along with issues of how to structure and manage its finances, ownership and distribution of wealth, and the consumption of its goods and services constitute "economics."

Reformed theology* theologically appraises economics and places it, with all other "realms," under the Lordship of God* in Jesus Christ*. It seeks conformity to the Kingdom of God* insofar as that is understood and can be a determinative direction for decisions and actions.

Two German social historians, Max Weber and Ernst Troeltsch, have been influential in perceptions of the ethos and cultural influences of Reformed Christianity (Calvinism*) and its theology on economics. The "Weber thesis" is that the Protestant and Reformed doctrine* of vocation* was transformative by establishing a religious significance to secular activities—making them a kind of "piety*" that fueled hard work* and financial gains in business and economics. Confidence in God's "election*" animates the moral life, according to Troeltsch. The "prevalence of the Weber thesis has generated a widespread perception that Reformed theology was instrumental in the rise of capitalism in early modern Europe" (*OHRT* 598). "Signs of election" were taken to be economic success and personal material/financial gain. This helped a "market economy" to develop and flourish.

The Weber thesis has been fully debated. Most clearly, Reformed theology/Calvinism's contribution to "capitalistic theory and practice over the centuries is undoubtedly partial, complex, a mixture of 'affinity' and antagonism" (*ERF* 113). Economics cannot inhabit an "autonomous sphere" to develop as it will since God is sovereign, rules in justice*, and demands care for the needs of the poor as well as the rich. Social responsibility, under God, is to be exhibited in economic practices to be truly oriented to God's kingdom.

Ecumenism

Visible expressions of the unity of the church* are in the cooperative efforts of Christian churches throughout the world, whatever their particular theological convictions, to recognize each other and work together in common cause for the purposes of the reign (Kingdom) of God* in the world. "Ecumenism" relates to the "whole household of God"—churches through the "inhabited earth" (Gr. *oikoumenē*). The essential unity of the church of Jesus Christ* is strengthened by individual churches looking beyond themselves to the common faith that unites them as disciples of Jesus Christ: "one Lord, one faith, one baptism*" (Eph. 4:5; see 4:1–13).

Reformed churches look to the ultimate unity of the church as they participate ecumenically, worldwide and in local contexts. Amy Pauw put it well when she wrote, "As members of the larger body of Christ, Reformed communities see their distinctives as contributions to the richness of the whole. No part of Christ's body may say to another part, 'I have no need of you' (1 Cor. 12:21). No single strand of Christian tradition* can claim historical or theological completeness. Reformed ecclesiology is rightly marked by a receptive ecumenism that seeks to respect and learn from other communities of Christian faith, even as it offers the witness of its own life" (*OHRT* 514).

Reformed theologians have been involved in ecumenical dialogues with other church communions, and "church fellowship" of Reformed churches with other church bodies, of varying theologies, has been a feature of the ecumenical movement for decades. These other churches include Lutheran, Baptist, Methodist, Mennonite, and Anglican bodies. Dialogues with Roman Catholic and Orthodox have led to better mutual understandings. Leaders in Reformed theology* have also been active in the World Council of Churches in various capacities.

Internal divisions over Reformed theology continue, yet ecumenical commitments remain.

Elders

Reformed theology* has highlighted the rule of the "elder" (Gr. *presbyteros*: "presbyter") as an ordained, permanent office in the church*. Elders are ordained for the functions of preaching*, teaching, and sacraments*, as well as for carrying out the government of the church (polity*).

A traditional distinction has been between "teaching" (pastors/teachers) and "ruling" elders (laity). In a congregation, the pastor and elected lay elders constitute the church session or consistory, which has responsibility for the corporate body and the church's ministries and programs. As one Reformed church puts it, "Ruling elders, together with teaching elders, exercise leadership, government, spiritual discernment, and discipline* and have responsibilities for the life of a congregation as well as the whole church, including ecumenical relationships" (*BO* G-2.0301).

The office of elder is rooted in Old and New Testament* "elders" who were leaders of the people of God*. Sixteenth-century Reformed churches, such as Geneva during John Calvin's* time, had the offices of elder and deacon*. This has been the ongoing traditional practice of Reformed churches holding the presbyterian form of church government. However, some churches have charged the elders with also carrying out the work* of deacons. In Congregational church polity, the office of deacon was discontinued.

Some Presbyterian denominations continue the practice of limiting elders only to men. In other churches, however, the office of ruling elder is open both to men and women church members. Those elected should be "persons of wisdom and maturity of faith*, having demonstrated skills in leadership and being compassionate in spirit. Ruling elders are so named not because they 'lord it over' the congregation (Matt. 20:25), but because they are chosen by the congregation to discern and measure its fidelity to the Word of God*, and to strengthen and nurture its faith and life" (*BO* G-2.0301).

Environment

Concern for and care of the environment is an urgent human responsibility. Reformed theology*, with its strong emphases on humanity* as created in the image of God* (Gen. 1:26–30) and that all creation* reflects God's glory and goodness, recognizes the obligation of the human family to use God's good gifts in creation in ways that protect, preserve, and treasure God's benevolent goodness in the created order.

The effects of sin* have moved humans to exploit the earth for human gain and often in human recklessness. Disregarding creation as a gift of God, lack of concern for creation care and protection of the environment has led to abuse and misuse of God's blessed creation. While humans have assumed they are "over nature" (Gen. 1:28), they have not honored the fact that we are also "under God," since God said, "See, I have given you . . ." (Gen. 1:29). All creation is God's and comes from God. We are to use God's gifts in light of God's graciousness to humanity.

In Reformed theology, "the fundamental claim that the earth is God's creation means that those who acknowledge the claim are bound to relate to the natural world with respect and care. 'God saw everything that [God] had made, and behold, it was very good' (Gen. 1:31). The creation has value simply because it is God's creation. And people who understand themselves as God's people cannot treat carelessly or destructively God's world, in which God delights" (Restoring 25).

An implication of this is that "God calls human beings, especially those who, following Jesus, accept stewardship* as servanthood. In faith* we discern God's new doing and hear the call to become involved with God in restoring creation, human and nonhuman" (Restoring 26). This mandate is urgent and pressing.

Eschatology

Theological events associated with the end of the world are subsumed under eschatology—the doctrine* of "last things." These have included the return of Christ; the millennium* (in pre-, post-, or a-millennial forms); the Resurrection*, and the Last Judgment*. On the personal level these embrace death* and heaven* and hell*.

All these point to the conviction that history* has a divine purpose and goal. Ultimately the Kingdom of God* is the end toward which we move. The final establishment of God's* reign over all things in Jesus Christ* is marked by the assurance to come that "at the name given to Jesus every knee should bend, in heaven and on earth and under the earth, and every tongue should confess that Jesus Christ is Lord, to the glory of God the Father" (Phil. 2:10–11). God will be "all in all" (1 Cor. 15:28). There will be "a new heaven and a new earth" (Rev. 21:1).

God's rule throughout the cosmos includes the ultimate blessedness of "the saints in the light" (Col. 3:12). Jürgen Moltmann* notes that Calvinist—and Reformed—theology "sees a continuity between *the grace* of Christ* experienced in history and *the glory of Christ* expected in the consummation" (*Coming* 271). "Christ rose again," said John Calvin*, "that he might have us as companions in the life to come" (*Inst.* 3.25.3). By grace, believers are "made perfectly blessed in the full enjoying of God to all eternity" (BC 7.038).

Living with the tension of the future realities of God's reign with the present, sinful world enables Christians to look to the power of the certain future, grounded in Christ's resurrection. Christians work* for transformation of political and social structures with a quest for social justice* assured of the coming kingdom and sustained by a "theology of hope*" (Moltmann).

Ethics, Social

The focusing of ethical reflection on social structures, social processes, or communities of persons may be designated "social ethics." Part of this also are the moral judgments and behavior found among groups of persons. These corporate concerns express a conviction of Reformed theology* that God* works among people and that the "people of God" are under obligation—in light of the Gospel of Jesus Christ*—to live corporately and socially according to the perspectives and commands of God's will.

Areas in which social ethics is especially pronounced are economics*, politics*, peace*, and justice*—in all their varied forms. Reformed churches, as bodies that express Reformed theological convictions, take part in bringing their theological views to bear on these areas of society. God's providence*, as an important Reformed understanding, means God is concerned with how people—and societies—live in the interactions among people. The church* seeks God's providential guidance and leading as it seeks to help societies move in ways congruent to understandings of who God is and what God desires.

At points, Reformed theology leads to countering entrenched powers in society, government, economics, and other societal powers when intentions and actions in these groups are counter to God's revelation* in Scripture* and the ethical postures required by the Gospel. The Theological Declaration of Barmen* provided a theological witness in the face of National Socialism in 1934 in Germany. Opposition to South Africa's unjust apartheid policies was a focus of the Confession of Belhar*. Theological witness accompanied by actions that seek to put "theology into practice" occur when various forms of social protests must be initiated to give voice to those with theological concerns.

Today, issues of political integrity and economic, racial, and environmental justice are focuses for Reformed social ethics. The needs of the poor and powerless are always main concerns.

Ethics, Theological

Theological ethics in Reformed theology* emerges from convictions that theological understandings ought to be put into "practice" in response to God's* revelation*, the teachings of Scripture*, and the guidance of the Holy Spirit*.

All life is to be lived in the presence of God and humans are to respond to God's will and way in the thoughts and actions of their lives. God's presence and power are pervasive realities that lead Christian persons to ground their activities and actions in understandings that lead them to believe what they do in service to God in Jesus Christ* is congruent with God's desires.

The Puritan William Ames spoke of theology as being composed of "faith* in God" and "observance toward God." Observance (Lat. *observantia*) is "the submissive performance of the will of God for the glory of God." The will of God is "a pattern and a rule, as shown by the words of Christ which both describe our observance." Our observance—as theological ethics—is "connected with service towards God, whence it is that *Obeying God and serving him* are one and the same thing." For "to do the will of God submissively is to serve God" (*Marrow* 219).

Theological ethics is an ongoing effort to serve God by understanding and acting as God wills. Among Puritans, theologians such as William Perkins and Ames wrote "Cases of Conscience," in which theological insights were brought to bear on ethical situations and decisions.

In contemporary culture, with its rapid changes, theological ethics faces ongoing challenges. Culture must be interpreted in all its varieties and dimensions. These interpretations must be considered in light of Scripture and theological understandings of the will of God. Vexing ethical problems of our time such as abortion, euthanasia, and personal decision-making in other arenas require responsible theological responses.

Evangelicalism

"Evangel" means "good news"—as does the word "Gospel." "Evangelicalism" has been a term for emphasizing the "good news" of the Christian Gospel and has taken various forms in different places.

The emergence of sixteenth-century Protestantism, over against Roman Catholicism, was an "evangelical" movement in that it sought to rediscover and rearticulate the Christian Gospel amid what its adherents believed were the false teachings of the Roman Church.

"Evangelical movements" in the mid-1700s included Pietism in Germany and Methodism in England. These were "a collection of loosely related movements marked by efforts to revitalize established churches that had lost spiritual vitality" (R&E x). Instead of church* authority*, the emphasis was on individuals, stressing conversion* and personal piety*.

In the United States, some Presbyterians and Reformed Christians accepted "Awakening" movements. Others rejected them. The larger evangelical movements in America included Reformed Christians. The main Presbyterian denomination had an Old School/New School schism (1837) over whether doctrinal and practical practices arising from the Awakenings were valid. For example, Old School adherents emphasized theology grounded in the Reformed tradition* which stressed education. Evangelicals downplayed the importance of theological traditions and often offered the slogan, "The Bible alone." This became interpreted as that "they should go back to the primitive practices of the New Testament* church, skipping over the history* that has intervened since then" (R&E xi).

Evangelicalism in later years has seen a number of strong leaders with authoritarian styles and abilities to sway popular opinion. Their reach has been beyond denominational churches, appealing to the religious experiences of ordinary people. Reformed churches interact with evangelical movements and some Reformed churches have left their denominations for others that are more "evangelically oriented." Otherwise, some converted through evangelical ministries may come to an appreciation for "more deeply grounded Reformed theology*" (R&E xii).

Evangelism

Traditionally, the mandate for evangelism has been drawn from Jesus's command to his disciples: "Go therefore and make disciples of all nations, baptizing them in the name of the Father and of the Son and of the Holy Spirit* and teaching them to obey everything that I have commanded you" (Matt. 28:19). The work of Christ's disciples is to spread the message of Jesus Christ* and his teachings, to "make disciples," and baptize in what became the "triune name" of God*: Father, Son, and Holy Spirit.

The church* witnesses to the Gospel message and Christ's Lordship over the world and in the lives of those who believe in him. This witness is launched by a concern for the lives of the world's people, who are all created in the image of God* (Gen. 1:27). Concerns are for their recognition of Jesus Christ as Lord and Savior as well as for their physical, mental, and social well-being. Holistic evangelism emphasizes the love of God for the whole of persons' lives.

Reformed theology* emphasizes a central dimension of the message of Christ: reconciliation* (2 Cor. 5:16–21). Reconciliation is concerned with "healing the enmities" which separate people from God and from each other (BC 9.31). The work of the Holy Spirit brings faith* in Christ (conversion*) and also brings reconciliation and healing.

Thus evangelism embraces a passionate desire to proclaim the Gospel message of Christ to foster faith while working for reconciliation in all facets of society. Jesus's own message was of the Kingdom (or reign) of God* that will ultimately be established. Faithful discipleship, in Reformed understandings, means a life of service to making Jesus Christ known and to working for peace*, justice*, and healing as expressions of God's kingdom desire in the here and now.

Extra-Calvinisticum

A contended issue of Christology* between Reformed and Lutheran theology in the Reformation period was the relation of the divine properties of Jesus Christ* during his incarnation*. This controversy is referred to by the name given by opponents to the Reformed view: the *extra-Calvinisticum*, or that "Calvinistic extra."

The Reformed held that Jesus Christ, the eternal Word of God* (John 1:1) and second person of the Trinity*, continues to be active and present "beyond the flesh" (Lat. *etiam extra carnem*) in and during his incarnation. The Reformed believed "the Word is fully united to but never totally contained within the human nature and, therefore, even in incarnation is to be conceived of as beyond or outside of (*extra*) the human nature" (*DLGTT* 111); in other words, Christ lost nothing of his divinity during his incarnation. He "retained his divine properties, including his immensity and omnipresence, in such a way that he was not confined or restricted to the form of the flesh that he took. Divinity was genuinely in union with humanity, and genuinely present in human physical form, but also transcendent of that form's finitude—present 'beyond' or 'outside' (*extra*) it as well" (*OHRT* 461).

Lutherans believed "the Logos was not beyond the flesh." They argued that there was nowhere the Logos was not present and not also united to the human nature of Christ. An omnipresent Logos (s.v. ubiquity*) could be really (if not locally) present with the elements in the Lord's Supper*.

Patristic and medieval theologians had affirmed what the Reformed taught. John Calvin* saw it as "marvelous" that Christ "descended from heaven* in such a way that, without leaving heaven, he willed to be borne in the virgin's womb, to go about the earth, and to hang upon the cross; yet he continuously filled the world even as he had done from the beginning!" (*Inst.* 2.13.4).

F

Faith

Faith is basic to Christian belief. Christian faith is belief and trust in God*, who is revealed in Scripture* and is personified in Jesus Christ*. John Calvin's* definition has been significant for Reformed theology*: Faith is "a firm and certain knowledge of God's benevolence toward us, founded upon the truth of the freely given promise in Christ, both revealed to our minds and sealed upon our hearts through the Holy Spirit*" (*Inst.* 3.2.7).

God is the object of faith. Scripture is the means by which God is made known and the way God's "benevolence" is known to humans. Reformed theology emphasizes that this benevolence is known in Jesus Christ. Christ brings salvation* and reconciliation* of sinful persons with God as from God's free grace* made known by the work of the Holy Spirit. The Westminster Confession* (1647) indicates that "the principal acts of saving faith are, accepting, receiving, and resting upon Christ alone for justification*, sanctification*, and eternal life, by virtue of the covenant* of grace" (BC 6.079).

Faith in Christ and union with Christ* bring salvation and new life and affects the whole person. "Faith," said William Ames, "is our life as it joins us to God" (*Marrow* 242). Christian life means serving God in the world through serving others. All actions are toward doing "everything to the glory of God" (1 Cor. 10:31).

While salvation is by faith, Reformed theology stresses the place of actions or "good works" in the Christian life. Faith expresses itself in good works—works of love, justice*, peace*, and all that gives glory to God. Ames wrote, "Faith which is without works is said to be dead (James 2:26). This is not because the life of faith flows from works but because works are subsequent acts necessarily flowing from the life of faith" (*Marrow* 254).

Faith and Reason

Human reason is something in which we put trust. Daily, we use our reason to give us answers and guide us in certain ways. Reason is the way we know ourselves and the world.

When it comes to knowing God*, reason has its place in Christian faith*. Reformed theologians have written about the knowledge of God* and probed the place of reason in relation to the other great source of our knowledge: faith. What is the relation between faith and reason?

Theologically, the Reformed have believed humans were created with reason "intact." John Calvin* said humanity* was created with "reason as guide, to distinguish what should be followed from what should be avoided" (Inst. 1.15.8). Reason helped direct life and would enable humans to mount up "even to God and eternal bliss." Reason could bring union with God.

But sin* entered. "Supernatural gifts were stripped" from humans, including "the light of faith as well as righteousness, which would be sufficient to attain heavenly life and eternal bliss" (Inst. 2.2.12). Humans are "banished from the Kingdom of God*" and can enter only by "the grace* of regeneration*."

Reason still exists. But it cannot bring a true knowledge of God—a knowledge that can bring union with God, or salvation*. Reason is corrupted in relation to divine things; though it can function as a guide for everyday life in "earthly things." A human is a "rational being"—"science" and arts are possible. But these are "inferior things" (Inst. 2.2.15).

Only faith, now, brings true knowledge of God and God's benevolence to our minds and hearts "through the work of the Holy Spirit*" (Inst. 3.2.7). Faith persuades the mind of what it does not comprehend, and gives certainty. Believers are "more strengthened by the persuasion of divine truth than instructed by rational proof" (3.2.14).

Federal Theology

Federal theology is sometimes called Covenant* theology (Lat. *foedus*: "covenant"). Reformed theology* in the sixteenth and seventeenth centuries developed the theme of "covenant" as a way of describing God's* relationship with humanity*, as expressed by numerous covenants of Scripture*, culminating in Jesus Christ*, who said, "This cup is the new covenant in my blood" (1 Cor. 11:25). Covenant or Federal theology became an organizing way of describing God's relationship to the people of Israel and to those who believe in Jesus Christ living by God's Law* and God's grace*.

Seventeenth-century Reformed theology, called Reformed Orthodoxy*, "saw federal or covenant theology as a redemptive-historical way of expressing substantially the same Reformation theology taught in their dogmatic works and confessional symbols" (CRO 404). Jesus Christ was central, and, as Heinrich Bullinger* developed covenantal thought, God was seen promising grace* to the people of Israel in anticipation of the covenant being fulfilled in Christ as the covenant of grace. This is a "history of salvation*" and "covenant" became a chief principle for interpreting Scripture and understanding God's role and rule in history*.

Some Reformed (Zacharias Ursinus, Caspar Olevianus) spoke of a "covenant of works," separate from and prior to the covenant of grace. This developed into seeing Adam as the "federal head" of all humanity with all who followed obliged to keep God's moral law. After Adam fell into sin* (Gen. 3), this way of salvation could not work, and God established the covenant of grace in which Christ fulfills the law—which humans cannot—and became the "federal head" of the covenant of grace.

The Puritans emphasized the practical importance of the covenant for personal piety*. The obligations of the covenant of grace were to lead to obedience to God and holiness of lives. Societally, obligations of charity and justice* were Christian duties.

Foreknowledge

An aspect of God's* knowledge is foreknowledge. Foreknowledge relates to things that will occur. It is a dimension of the omniscience of God, who, as the Psalmist wrote, knows completely "even before a word is on my tongue" (Ps. 139:4).

John Calvin* spoke of this when he wrote that "when we attribute foreknowledge to God, we mean that all things always were, and perpetually remain, under his eyes, so that to his knowledge there is nothing future or past, but all things are present" (*Inst.* 3.21.5). Amandus Polanus indicated that "God knows simultaneously in one act of his understanding all things that are for us past, present, and future" (*Syntagma* 1012A, in GMG 207). Put formally, Polanus wrote, "The foreknowledge of God signifies God as having foreseen and foreknown from eternity all things that are said to be future with respect to us" (1013C, in GMG 207). In his detailed treatment, Polanus introduced two sets of distinctions: Foreknowledge is universal or particular, and either theoretical or practical.

These descriptions do not promote fatalism or determinism. For foreknowledge does not exclude human freedom* and responsibility. The Westminster Confession* (1647) states, "Although in relation to the foreknowledge and decree* of God, the first cause, all things come to pass immutably and infallibly, yet, by the same providence*, he ordereth them to fall out according to the nature of second causes, either necessarily, freely, or contingently" (BC 6.025). God knows what God wills directly and immediately. Some things are willed only indirectly and emerge as human free choice, which interacts or responds to secondary causality—things that occur in relation to each other during time.

Reformed theologians always indicate that humans have freedom to make choices and thus have responsibilities for their actions. God's will (foreordination) is accomplished in relation to human freedom.

Forgiveness

Early Christian creeds* confess: "I believe in the forgiveness of sins*" (BC 1.3, 2.3). This is a basic element in the church's* faith* and in the faith of each Christian.

Reformed theology* sees forgiveness of sins as part of the experience of salvation* and reconciliation* with God*. It is a result of the justification* of sinners who receive forgiveness of sin and a new status before God on the basis of God's grace* and the work of Jesus Christ*. Forgiveness is received in faith. The barrier of sin between sinner and God is removed and the power of sin is broken. Believers live and serve God in Christ by the power of the Holy Spirit*. The comprehensiveness of forgiveness of sins is indicated by the Heidelberg Catechism (1563): "I believe that God, because of Christ's satisfaction, will no longer remember any of my sins or my sinful nature which I need to struggle against all my life. Rather, by grace God grants me the righteousness of Christ to free me forever from judgment*" (BC 4.056).

Forgiveness of sins in Jesus Christ brings recognition that Christ is "God's mighty claim upon our whole life," said the Theological Declaration of Barmen* (1530; BC 8.14). This work of the Holy Spirit enables persons to "receive forgiveness as they forgive one another and to enjoy the peace* of God [Rom. 5:1] as they make peace among themselves" (9.20). The Spirit enables forgiven persons "to respond in faith, repentance*, and obedience, and initiates the new life in Christ" (9.21). Forgiven people are to live, practicing that "as the Lord has forgiven you, so you also must forgive" (Col. 3:13; cf. Eph. 4:32). This new life in forgiveness, lived out in the church, includes the call to "practice forgiveness of enemies" (BC 9.45).

Forgiveness of sins liberates Christians and the church to live as forgiven people.

Free Will

"Free will" has been a contested issue in the history* of theology. The term has been used in different ways, adding to its ambiguities.

When used to describe the power to act or decide, the phrase rejects a determinism in which humans become "puppets" who have no free choice or responsibility for their actions.

Reformed theology* follows Augustine in his controversy with Pelagius and semi-Pelagians. Do humans have the power of free will, freely to choose to love and serve God* or to come to faith* in Jesus Christ? Reformed theology emphasizes the power of human sin* to corrupt human nature, so all human powers have sinful roots. This includes the human will. The effects of "original sin*" means humans do not have the ability or "will" in themselves to "choose" to respond to God, since the will always acts in accord with the nature of the one who acts. The Westminster Confession* (1647) said that humans by their "fall into a state of sin, hath wholly lost all ability of will to any spiritual good accompanying salvation*" (BC 6.061).

What has been lost for sinful humans is free choice. Specifically, this is "the ability freely to choose the good and freely to avoid what is evil" (DLGTT 177). Only God through the Holy Spirit* can bring grace* and the gift of faith to provide salvation. The Spirit brings a sinner into God's grace and brings freedom* from the "natural bondage under sin" to enable a believer "freely to will and to do that which is spiritually good" (BC 6.062). "New life" includes a new will.

Christian believers now have "free will" to do the good—serve God. But Christians still sin. Freedom can be used in sinful ways. Complete freedom to do good alone occurs only in the state of glory.

Freedom

Freedom applies to several dimensions of Reformed theology*.

God's* freedom is the divine freedom in which God is God and is free to will whatever God desires with no coercion or influence of outside forces. As William Ames said, God's will is "truly free, because whatever it wills it wills not by necessity of nature but by counsel. It is most free, completely and absolutely free, depending on nothing else" (*Marrow* 97). God's "sovereignty" is God's total freedom. The expression of God's will in God's "decrees*" carries the divine freedom. God's actions are "utterly free, absolute, and inalterable" and are "predicated upon nothing but the nature of the divine essence" (*DLGTT* 88). God is free. Karl Barth* argued that the incarnation* expressed God's freedom for humans and defined God as "the One who loves in freedom" (*CD* II/1, §28).

Human freedom can mean different things. Theologically, the Reformed have aligned with Augustine in recognizing the stages of human freedom. In their creation*, humans had freedom and were "able to sin*." After sin entered (Gen. 3), they were "not able not to sin." With redemption in Jesus Christ*, they are "able not to sin." In heavenly glory they will be "not able to sin."

Christian freedom is seen in relation to God's Law*. The law condemns sinners who cannot obey the law as God desires. John Calvin* noted that Christians who are justified by faith* in Jesus Christ, who are still liable to sin and who remain imperfect, are now—because of Christ's saving death*—freed from being "slaves to sin" (Rom. 6:15–23). The law no longer condemns. Now Christians have freedom for obedience to God, in Christ. The law now guides Christians in following God's will (*Inst.* 2.7.12). Now Christians "through love become enslaved to one another" (Gal. 5:13).

Fundamentalism

Fundamentalism is an American movement dating from the early twentieth century. It seeks to defend Protestant Christianity in the face of the challenges posed by theological liberalism, higher biblical criticism, evolution, and other emerging cultural trends. George Marsden said, "A fundamentalist is an evangelical who is angry about something" (cited in R&E 279).

The 1920s Fundamentalist/Modern Controversy was a conflict to unite conservative Christians in saving their denominations from the growth of Modernist theology. Modernism sought to update traditional Christian faith* in light of new advances in science, history*, biblical studies, and social sciences. Presbyterians in the northern United States were especially involved. A central event was the 1925 Scopes Monkey Trial in Dayton, Tennessee, where Presbyterian William Jennings Bryan led a campaign and argued a court case seeking to curtail the teaching of biological education in public schools. John Scopes was found guilty of teaching evolution, but national press coverage ridiculed Bryan (who died shortly thereafter) and pictured Fundamentalism as a function of rural ignorance, to be overpowered by urban and cosmopolitan cultures.

The movement began with publication of The Fundamentals (1910–1915), ninety essays on "the fundamentals of Christianity," originally a series of booklets supported by two wealthy Presbyterian brothers, Lyman and Milton Stewart. Three editors followed and more than three million booklets were distributed. A number of Reformed and Presbyterian writers participated, including B. B. Warfield of Princeton Theological Seminary, a traditional bastion of Reformed Orthodoxy*. Presbyterian Princeton professor J. Gresham Machen, in his Christianity and Liberalism (1923), argued that theological liberalism and Christianity were two different religions. The reorganization of Princeton Seminary in 1929 reflected the diversity of the Presbyterian denomination and led to the departure of Machen and others.

A "new evangelicalism*" emerged from the late 1940s, but divided Fundamentalist movements continue within various Reformed denominations as well as in denominations with explicitly Fundamentalist convictions.

~

G

Gender and Sexuality

Issues of gender and sexuality have been the focus of much debate within Reformed churches. Debates have been based on interpretations of Scripture* and theological convictions as understood in various strands of Reformed theology*.

Many Reformed denominations continue to support traditional understandings of church* practices about marriage and ordination* and officeholders in churches. They believe marriage must be between a man and a woman and that those who are LGBTQ+ should not be ordained to offices in the church, including as ministers (pastors), elders*, and deacons*. Biblical and theological convictions are the bases for these perspectives.

Other Reformed denominations—particularly the United Church of Christ and the Presbyterian Church (U.S.A.)—have expressed other viewpoints. In 2011, the PC(USA) amended its *Book of Order* to the effect that "persons in a same-gender relationship may be considered for ordination and/or installation as deacons, ruling elders, and teaching elders (ministers of the Word and Sacrament). Also, Ordaining bodies (sessions and presbyteries) are permitted but not required to ordain lesbian, gay, bisexual, or transgender persons. Candidates for ordination and/or installation must be considered as individuals on a case-by-case basis; it is not permissible to establish a policy that excludes a category of persons in the abstract" (see "Sexuality and Same-Gender Relationships," at https://www.presbyterianmission.org /what-we-believe/sexuality-and-same-gender-relationships/).

In 2015, the PC(USA) enacted changes with the effects that "responsibility for decisions about whether and where to have a marriage service is granted to teaching elders and commissioned ruling elders, and to sessions. Pastors are responsible for deciding whether they will or will not officiate at a marriage service. Sessions are responsible for deciding whether the church's property may be used for a marriage service."

The United Church of Christ has affirmed "equal marriage rights for couples regardless of gender" (see "Marriage Equality and LGBTQ Rights," at https://www.ucc.org/marriage_equality_and_lgbtq_rights/) and has no gender/sexuality restrictions on ministers and lay leadership in churches.

General Assembly

The highest governing body (judicatory) of Reformed denominations that have a Presbyterian polity* or church* government is the General Assembly. The Assembly represents a unity with the three lower levels of representative church "courts": synods*, presbyteries, and sessions of churches. The highest body in some denominations is called the National Synod or Synod, with lower bodies called Colloquies, Classes, or Consistories. The French Reformed Church organized the first National Synod in 1559 and established a book of discipline*. This laid a foundation for a developing Presbyterianism.

The Assembly features equal numbers of ministers (teaching elders*, ministers of Word and Sacrament) with ruling elders. Together they are "Commissioners" and represent all Presbyteries of the denomination. Commissioners are elected by the presbyteries and not by local congregations. The Assembly elects a Moderator for a term between assemblies. An elected stated clerk is the chief executive officer for the denomination.

The Assembly does the work* of the church in hearing reports from committees, church boards, and other entities which carry out the church's mission. The Assembly can review decisions of lower governing bodies. It debates issues and may make pronouncements that speak to the church as a whole. The Assembly also maintains ecumenical relationships with other church bodies.

Some decisions of a General Assembly have the force of church law when all the established procedures have been followed. Other times, the General Assembly sends issues or resolution to presbyteries for a denominational vote. If the vote is positive from a majority of the presbyteries, the issue is then voted upon by the next General Assembly to become operative.

Traditionally, the General Assembly has met annually. Now, some meet biennially. The American Reformed tradition* has emphasized the concept that powers undelegated in the church's constitution remain with the presbyteries and not with the General Assembly.

God

God is the supreme being, Creator and ruler of the universe.

Reformed theology* realizes, said William Ames, that "God, as he is in himself, cannot be understood by any save himself." So "the things which pertain to God must be explained in a human way," and "because they are explained in our way for human comprehension, many things are spoken of God according to our own conceiving rather than according to his real nature" (*Marrow* 83; cf. Accommodation).

In line with Christian tradition*, Amandus Polanus defined God as "an uncreated spirit, existing from himself, one in essence, and three in the persons of the Father, Son and Holy Spirit*" (*Syntagma* 857A, in GMG 109). Reformed theologians, as well as Reformed confessions* of the Reformation and post-Reformation period, went on to distinguish, for discussion's sake, "the essence of God . . . the attributes of God . . . the Trinity* . . . of God, and the works of God." Richard A. Muller indicates that Reformed scholastics defined God as "the infinite, uncreated, self-existent, and necessary Spirit, one in essence and three in person, Father, Son, and Spirit, the eternal Creator, Preserver, and Redeemer of all things" (*DLGTT* 90; cf. Trinity).

By the eighteenth and nineteenth centuries, Reformed theology began to stress God's immanent and personal nature. Revivalism and the experience of God's graciousness were held together by Jonathan Edwards, while theologians at Princeton Seminary, notably Charles Hodge, continued to stress traditional Reformed approaches. Friedrich Daniel Ernst Schleiermacher* stressed human experience and appropriation of a God-consciousness in a "feeling of absolute dependence" (*CF* 1 §4, 1:22).

Karl Barth's* *Church Dogmatics* emphasizes the Word of God* (vol. 1), the Doctrine of God (vol. 2), the Doctrine of Creation (vol. 3), and the Doctrine of Reconciliation (vol. 4). Barth believed "the doctrine* of the Trinity is what basically distinguishes the Christian doctrine of God as Christian" (*CD* I/1, 301). He emphasized God as "the one who loves in freedom*" (*CD* II/1, 257).

Government, Civil

Reformed theology* has recognized the importance of civil government in the work of God*.

All societies need governing structures so laws can be administered and civil order established and maintained. For John Calvin*, the duties of church* and state are distinct and should not be comingled. Each entity has responsibilities, with civil government being responsible, under God, for "the establishment of civil justice* and outward morality" (*Inst.* 4.20.1). Calvin was concerned that equity and care for the poor be established while citizens live in peace* (4.20.9).

"Magistrates"—and civil government itself—are established by God. Magistrates have responsibilities as "vicars of God" who "have been ordained ministers of divine justice" (*Inst.* 4.20.6). They function as "God's deputies."

Different forms of government have their own usefulness. Whatever governmental form is adopted in a society, the "judicial law" nations practice for citizens should be led by "certain formulas of equity and justice, by which they might live together blamelessly and peaceably." Every nation "should be left free to make such laws as it foresees to be profitable for itself. Yet these must be in conformity to that perpetual rule of love, so that they indeed vary in form but have the same purpose" (*Inst.* 4.20.15).

Against Anabaptist views, the Reformed have recognized the freedom* of Christians to use law courts and litigation. But litigation must be carried out without hatred and revenge. While one may "go to law with a brother, one is not therewith allowed to hate him, or be seized with a mad desire to harm him, or hound him relentlessly" (*Inst.* 4.20.17).

Civil government may use "the power of the sword" and wage war (BC 6.127). Obedience is due the government, but this obedience may never lead to disobedience to the Lord, who is "the King of Kings" (*Inst.* 4.20.32).

Grace

Grace is God's* unconditional blessing to humanity* to maintain human life (common grace) and bring salvation* and perseverance* in the life of faith* (special grace).

Reformed theology* acknowledges God's Lordship over all—the natural world and human life. God desires to maintain life and enable sinful persons to live in societies. God restrains the power of sin*, which would bring ruin. God sustains life so blessings can be experienced and the whole creation* can function. God permits natural gifts to flourish. Arts and sciences exist as God's "excellent gifts" (*Inst.* 2.2.12–17). This is God's "general grace" or "common grace."

God's "special grace" relates to salvation. God chooses to provide salvation and faith for persons, forgiving sin through the death* of Jesus Christ* (justification*). God gives the gift of faith by the Holy Spirit* so the "people of God" (in Reformed understanding: the "elect") can love and serve God in the church* and live for the glory of God. They follow the way of Jesus Christ as they grow in faith (sanctification*).

Salvation is by God's grace, received in faith. Karl Barth* said, "It is by grace and *only* by grace that we are accepted by God" (*HCT* 92). Grace is "the sum of the gospel" (*CD* II/2, 13). Jesus Christ himself is God's grace. "Grace is the distinctive mode of God's being in so far as it seeks and creates fellowship by its own free inclination and favor" (*CD* II/2, 353). No human unworthiness hinders God's grace.

The grace of God is the marvelous message of the Christian Gospel. Said Barth: "Despite God's holiness, Grace! Despite human sin, Peace*!" (*EE* 77). The only answer to grace is gratitude: "Grace and gratitude belong together. . . . Grace evokes gratitude like the voice an echo. Gratitude follows grace like thunder lightning" (*CD* IV/1, 41).

H

Heaven

Believers in Jesus Christ* find their eternal destination in heaven. The elect receive eternal rest in heaven, where joy never ends and the worship* and praise of God* redounds forever.

Heaven is the "invisible" portion of creation*. While the "visible" portion is accessible to humans, heaven is not accessible until after death*. Heaven is the eternal abode of God, to which Jesus Christ ascended (Heb. 9:24), and is where the fullness of the triune God is found on the "throne of grace*" (Heb. 4:16). Angels surround the throne in worship of God (Rev. 7:11).

Reformed theology* rejects the traditional Roman Catholic view of Purgatory as a place where the souls of the faithful dead are "purified" before entering heaven. John Calvin* wrote *Psychopannychia* (1534) against the Anabaptist view of "soul sleep," where souls await the final resurrection*. The Westminster Confession* (1647) speaks of souls after death neither dying nor sleeping and "having an immortal subsistence, immediately return to God who gave them. The souls of the righteous, being then made perfect in holiness, are received into the highest heavens, where they behold the face of God in light and glory" (*BC* 6.177).

The heavenly "city" is where "the glory of God is its light" (Rev. 21:23, 25). The "throne of God and of the Lamb will be in it, and his servants will worship him" (Rev. 22:3). This is an ultimate, eternal blessing. What glory awaits!

This vision of heaven affects Christian life. Calvin urged "Meditation on the Future Life" (*Inst.* 3.9). This meditation keeps us from loving earthly things too much. It helps us not have an immoderate fear of death. It urges us to live in faith* and obedience. Ultimately, the saints will be elevated to the Lord's "sublime fellowship," as God will "deign to make them sharers in his happiness" (*Inst.* 3.9.6).

Hell

Traditionally, heaven* is the state of the "blessed," the elect in Christ. Hell is the state of those "outside" Christ (reprobate), which is the state of eternal punishment. God's* justice* and the sinful depravity of humanity* have been seen as necessitating hell. As the Westminster Confession* (1647) put it, "The souls of the wicked are cast into hell, where they remain in torments and utter darkness, reserved to the judgment* of the great day" (BC 6.177; cf. 7.196, 199).

Hell is the place for "the extreme torment of sin*, Rev. 21:8," wrote William Ames. There, "pains and the greatest agony of soul and body occur, Luke 16:23," and "there are lamentations, howling, gnashing of teeth and similar marks of greatest agony, Luke 13:28." "But," continued Ames, "concerning the place of hell and the manner of torture and the nature of the attendant circumstances, the Scripture* has said nothing definite, because it is not necessary for us to know" (Marrow 126–27).

In the nineteenth and twentieth centuries, some Reformed theologians moved away from this traditional Reformed picture of hell. Friedrich Daniel Ernst Schleiermacher* taught a universalism*. His emphasis was seeing the destiny of all persons as determined in Jesus Christ* and thus not dividing the human race into "elect" and "reprobate."

Karl Barth* recast the doctrine* of election*. Jesus Christ took the place of the absolute divine decree*, and Christ himself became the "object" of election as well as the "subject" of election. Election is "the sum of the Gospel" which declares from first to last the "yes" of God and not the "no" (CD II/2, 13). Barth continued, "We actually know of only one certain triumph of hell—the handing-over of Jesus—and that this triumph of hell took place in order that it would never again be able to triumph over anyone" (II/2, 496).

Heresy

"Heresy" is from the Greek term *hairesis*, meaning "choice." Heresy is a view that is chosen instead of the official teachings of the Christian church*. This is a conscious choice and in the eyes of the church sets one as being wrong as well as potentially spreading danger by inducing others to believe in the heretical teaching. So heresy has been taken very seriously by the church.

Early church struggles to establish what became Christian orthodoxy on key doctrines*, such as "Who is God*?" (Trinity*) and "Who is Jesus Christ*?" (Christology*), meant careful attention was given to the verbal formulations of these teachings by various Christians. When official Christian teachings became set—with councils such as Nicaea (AD325; Trinity) and the Chalcedonian formula (451; Christology)—unorthodox views could be considered "heresy."

In Reformed theology* and church confessional writings, warnings against heresy appear. In Geneva, under John Calvin*, Michael Servetus lost his life for his views on the Trinity. Heinrich Bullinger* warned against heresies on the Trinity in the Second Helvetic Confession (1566; BC 5.019). Calvin looked back to Augustine and said, "Heretics, although they preach the name of Christ, have herein no common ground with believers," for "we will find Christ among the heretics in name only, not in reality" (*Inst.* 2.15.1). He continued with Augustine's understanding that "heretics corrupt the sincerity of the faith* with false dogmas" (4.2.5).

Some Reformed confessions* enjoin magistrates to "suppress stubborn heretics (who are truly heretics), who do not cease to blaspheme the majesty of God and to trouble, and even to destroy the Church of God" (BC 5.255; cf. 6.123, 6.130).

The Theological Declaration of Barmen* (1934) warned against the "false doctrine*" of "German Christians." In the 1980s, the World Alliance of Reformed Churches declared apartheid in South Africa a matter of heresy.

History

Lord Eustace Percy wrote that in his *Institutes* John Calvin* had expressed "something much more explosive than the dogma of predestination*; [the *Institutes*] contained a philosophy of history, a statement of Christian faith* in terms of divine purpose" (*John Knox* 109).

Calvin's doctrine* of providence* relates to God's* continuing interaction with the world, humans, and human history. God's sovereignty entails God not as one who "idly observes from heaven what take[s] place on earth, but as keeper of the key, he governs all events. Thus it pertains no less to his hands than to his eyes" (*Inst.* 1.16.4).

Reformed theology* speaks of God's "general providence," by which God oversees the universe, sustaining and governing it through human history, and God's "special providence," in which God directs the lives of individuals, exercising "especial care" (1.16.4).

This means the working out of historical processes is not of human purposes, but God's purposes. Persons are important because they are agents and means through which God's purposes for history are carried out. All persons, everywhere, are agents of God's purposes.

Providence is "without," in terms of the big, overall arc of history, as human history moves toward the ultimate Kingdom of God*. Providence is "within," as God works within the lives of all persons as they live out the history and purposes for which they were created by their Creator. God is transcendent, over and beyond all history and historical processes. Yet God is also immanent within historical processes, as God's will and plan is carried out in and through human history.

Seventeenth-century English Puritans had Calvin's lively view of God's providence, and as they participated within the history of their times, they realized they were part of the history in which God was at work. This brought confidence and hope*.

Holy Spirit

The Holy Spirit is the third member of the Trinity*, along with God* the Father and God the Son.

The Nicene Creed affirms the Spirit as "the Lord, the giver of life." The Spirit "proceeds from the Father and the Son" (in contrast to Eastern Christianity, which teaches the "single procession" of the Spirit only from the Father). The Spirit shares the same "substance" as the Father and the Son, and "with the Father and Son is worshiped and glorified" (BC 1.3).

Reformed theology* sees the robust work of the Holy Spirit in the world, throughout the creation*. The Spirit is active in relation to Scripture*, leading persons to recognize Scripture as the Word of God*. The Spirit conveys faith* in Jesus Christ* as one's Lord and Savior. John Calvin* wrote that "faith is the principal work of the Holy Spirit." The Spirit is "the key that unlocks for us the treasures of the Kingdom of Heaven*" through the Spirit's "illumination" (Inst. 3.1.4). By the "secret energy of the Spirit," believers "come to enjoy Christ and all his benefits," for the Spirit is "the bond by which Christ effectually unites us to himself" (3.1.1). The Spirit is active in the calling* of the elect (BC 6.064) and gathers the church* as the "people of God" and the "body of Christ" (Rom. 8:14).

The Spirit is active in sanctification* as the Spirit with the Word and dwells in the church's life and in the lives of believers. The Spirit is "our teacher in prayer*, to tell us what is right and temper our emotions" (Inst. 3.20.5). Without the Spirit, "the sacraments* profit not a whit." By the Spirit, sacraments strengthen and enlarge faith (3.14.9). The Spirit endows the church with gifts for ministry* (BC 9.38).

The Spirit empowers believers "to live holy and joyful lives" (BC 11.4).

Hope

God* is "the God of hope." Christian believers "abound in hope by the power of the Holy Spirit*" (Rom. 15:13). For "hope is a virtue which leads us to expect things which God has promised us, Rom. 8:25" (*Marrow* 245).

William Ames spoke for Reformed theology* when he wrote that "hope is grounded in God's promises." Christian hope "looks to the grace* of God and Christ as the only sources of good to be bestowed. 1 Peter 1:13; Col. 1:27" (*Marrow* 246). God graciously promises hope, which "looks to all the things which faith* sees in the promises of God." God's promises are sure and God brings them to pass. Believers can have "great certainty" God's promises will be fulfilled, even as we wait "with patience" (Rom. 8:25).

Hope "looks mainly towards eternal life," grounded in God's Old Testament* promises (*Inst.* 3.25.1–3, 2.10–17) seen in God's faithfulness in the cross of Jesus Christ*, even as tribulation is endured with patience and obedience (3.8.3–4).

Jürgen Moltmann* emphasized that "the Christian hope for the future comes of observing a specific, unique event—that of the resurrection* and appearing of Jesus Christ. . . . Hence to recognize the resurrection of Christ means to recognize in this event the future of God for the world and the future which [humans] find in this God and his acts" (*TOH* 194). Christ's resurrection is basis for "the resurrection of us all," said John Calvin* (*Inst.* 3.25.3).

The "effect of hope is a confirmation of the soul as a *Safe and firm anchor*, Heb. 6:19," wrote Ames. On this, Calvin said: "The truth of God is a chain for binding us to Himself, so that no distance of place and no darkness may hinder us from cleaving to Him. . . . Even though we have to contend with continual storms, we are safe from the danger of shipwreck" (CNTC 12:86).

Humanity

There are two great initial truths about humanity which Reformed theology* affirms. The most basic thing is that humans are created in "the image of God*" (Gen. 1:27). All persons owe their existence to the creative act of God. This implies the relationship between God and humanity is essential to human existence. The Adam and Eve story of Genesis 1 indicates the communication, dependence, and relationship of trust and love* that God intends for humanity.

The second dimension of humanity is sinfulness. Genesis 3 is the story of disobedience to God's commands and the human desire to be at the center of life, putting themselves ahead of following what God wishes. This is "original sin*," meaning humans are sinful in their "origins." Reformed theology speaks starkly of this condition: In "original sin, the image of God was utterly defaced in man, and he and his children became by nature hostile to God, slaves to Satan, and servants to sin*" (BC 3.03). This leads to physical death* and spiritual death as separation from God (Rom. 3:23; 6:23). The sinful nature of humanity leads to actual sins, acts that are sinful. Some sinful acts are "more serious than others" (BC 5.039).

The Good News of the Christian Gospel is that while humans cannot, by their own actions, forgive their sins and establish a relationship of love and trust, God has sent Jesus Christ* to be the Savior, Deliverer, and Redeemer of those God will save by giving the gift of salvation* and reconciliation* through faith* in Christ. Jesus gave "his life for the sins of the world" (BC 11.2). Jesus's resurrection* from the dead broke "the power of sin and evil, delivering us from death to life eternal."

Redeemed humanity can fulfill their "chief end": "to glorify God and to enjoy him forever" (BC 7.001).

Hymnody

Early Reformed Christians praised God* through scriptural songs that were predominantly metrical versions of the Psalms. Psalters, which collected these Psalms, began to be published in Geneva and grew to a completed volume of 150 psalms with 125 tunes (1564).

Among the Puritans in England, significant collections of Psalms were published. Thomas Sternhold and John Hopkins produced *The Whole Booke of Psalmes, collected into Englysh metre* (1562), which provided worship* resources for congregations.

The English Congregationalist Isaac Watts argued for the need of Reformed congregations to give voice to their praise of God in human language, instead of exclusively in the language of Scripture*. Reformed Christians used the Psalms alone because they believed God should be praised in God's own language—the biblical language of the Psalms. Controversies in the United States about whether praise "of human origin" (hymns) were proper for worship split some congregations. Watts's *Hymns and Spiritual Songs* (1707) used scriptural language and images that were adapted to the "mind of the living church*."

Reformed hymn writers of note, such as Philip Doddridge, William Cowper, and John Newton, supplemented Watts's materials. As many Reformed churches sanctioned the use of hymns for worship, hymnals were produced for congregational use. Through the years, hymnody has been updated to reflect various contextual dimensions while preserving hymnody's basic purpose of praising God.

The Confession of 1967 notes that "Confessional statements have taken such varied forms as hymns . . ." (*BC* 9.02). Throughout, the confession notes that "the church gathers to praise God" (9.36) and that "the church responds to the message of reconciliation in praise and prayer*" (9.50). Hymnody is a primary means of praise. Music contributes to a "Christian congregation" when it helps worshippers "look beyond themselves to God and to the world," which is the object of God's love (9.50).

~

I

Idolatry

The Heidelberg Catechism (1563) defines idolatry as "having or inventing something in which one trusts in place of or alongside of the only true God*, who has revealed himself in the Word" (BC 4.095; cf. 5.020). While making "idols" ("graven image," KJV) in "the form of any figure" is forbidden in the God's Law* (Exod. 20:4; Deut. 4:16, 23, 25), it is clear that Reformed theology* recognizes that almost any "thing" can become an "idol." When this happens, sin* occurs.

"Idols" take away our trust in God. They give "something else" the same status of God—who is to be our supreme Lord, the true God to whom all worship*, obedience, and love is to be given (1 Cor. 10:14; 1 John 5:21).

Material representations of God violate Reformed convictions that God is utterly transcendent. In the sixteenth century, this led to rejection of Roman Catholic venerations of images in worship and "relics." By extension, some Reformed considered armed resistance to rulers who were considered "idolatrous." Christian magistrates were to "root out" idolatry to keep the purity of the church* (BC 5.253; cf. 3.24).

The church is led by the Holy Spirit* "to unmask idolatries in Church and culture" (BC 11.4). This means all Christians must be alert and perceptive to what practices in church and culture may be functioning in idolatrous manners. One dimension of this can be political idolatry—the elevation of various ideologies, nationalisms, or leaders that can be put alongside God as objects of trust and obedience. This is what the Confessing Church of Germany pointed toward in the Theological Declaration of Barmen* (1934) when it rejected a state that could "become the single and totalitarian order of human life" (BC 8.23).

Idolatry can be defined as "absolutizing a proximate good." Whatever "takes the place of God" as Lord is idolatry.

Image of God

Biblical accounts of the creation* of humanity* indicate not only that God* is the Creator of all persons but that humanity itself is created "in the image of God" (Gen. 1:26–28; Lat. *imago Dei*). This shows a connection between humanity and its Creator going beyond that God "breathed into his nostrils the breath of life, and the man became a living being" (Gen. 2:7). In some way, created humanity has/is/exhibits the "image of God."

The image of God is a basic link between humans and their Creator. But there have been numerous interpretations of the meaning of the "image of God." A dominant theme has seen the image as referring to the rational nature of humans (Aquinas). Humans can use their reason* and thus reflect the divine *logos* or "reason" by which God created the world. Yet this can make humans primarily "intellects."

Some have seen the image as meaning dominion over the earth. God exercises power and dominion—so can humans. Yet this view can lead to the exploitation and destruction of nature.

The image as human freedom* has had its proponents. Humans have "freedom" and creativity—as does God. Yet this can devolve into self-gratification when freedom is selfishly used.

Reformed theologian Daniel L. Migliore suggests the "image of God" symbol is to describe "human life in relationship with God and with other creatures." For "to be human is to live freely and gladly in relationships of mutual respect and love." This reflects God who "lives" not as solitary, "but in communion." Humans are to live not for themselves, but in relationships with others—with all others, as does God. In this way, "image of God" can turn from noun to verb: Humans are "to image God" (*Faith Seeking* 141). Then they become the humans God intends.

Incarnation

Reformed theology* has affirmed the teachings of the early church* and creeds* on the person of Jesus Christ*. In him, the eternal second person of the Trinity* became a human being and "assumed flesh." Basic is the conviction that "the Word became flesh and lived among us" (John 1:14).

Jesus Christ was one person with two natures: divine and human (BC 5.062, 5.064, 6.044, 6.045). Jesus was both fully divine and fully human. It was necessary for Jesus Christ in his work of salvation* in dying on the cross to be divine so his death* could have the power to effect reconciliation* of God* and humans through the forgiveness* of sin*. It was necessary for Christ to be human so he could identify fully with human persons in taking their sins upon himself (1 John 3:5). Karl Barth* wrote that "the God who acts and speaks in Jesus Christ expresses his own true divinity precisely in his true humanity" (CD IV/3/2, 763). Further, Christ's "death on the cross was and is the fulfillment of the incarnation of the Word and therefore the humiliation of the Son of God and exaltation of the Son of Man" (IV/2, 140–41). As P. T. Forsyth said, in Jesus Christ, God "gave us Himself—His life, His action" (Revelation 10).

Reformed theology affirms the "communication of properties" (Lat. communication idiomatum). This refers to the ways the properties of each of Christ's natures are "communicated" or interchanged in the unity of Christ's person. Thus what can be said of Christ's humanity can be said of his divinity, and vice versa. This meant that all the attributes, together, belonged to the "whole Christ"—to Jesus Christ according to both his natures. In its emphases, Reformed Christology* was closer to the Antiochene than to the Alexandrian Christology of the early church.

Infralapsarianism

After the death* of John Calvin* in 1564, Reformed theologians considered questions relating to the eternal ordering of the divine decree(s)*. Two viewpoints emerged. Both agreed that God* ordered all things and brought them to pass according to the divine will and divine decrees.

The issue was: What was in the mind of God as God established plans for all things and persons? The views were called supralapsarianism* and infralapsarianism. Was the eternal decree to elect persons to salvation* made *prior to* or *after* the eternal decree to create humanity* and permit the fall into sin*?

The infralapsarian view (from Lat. *infra lapsum*) was that the eternal decree to elect some for salvation was made after or posterior to the decree of election*. This meant the object of the election decree is all elect humans. They are considered, in eternity, to be created and fallen into sin. They need salvation and redemption. The sequence would thus be: creation*, permission of the fall into sin, and election/salvation. Election is of fallen, sinful human beings. "Reprobation*"—of the nonelect—was seen to be God's "passing over" of this portion of humanity, leaving them in their sins and eternity in hell*. The supralapsarian* view taught that God first decreed election and reprobation before decreeing the fall into sin.

The infralapsarian position has been the dominant view in most Reformed confessions*. This was the position of the Westminster Confession* (1647) and the Synod of Dordt (1618–1619). For Dordt, the elect are said to be elected "out of the entire human race fallen" (*Landmark* 182).

Dordt did not contend or exclude the supralapsarian position. The differing viewpoints created theological controversies in Reformed theology*. But the issue was not definitively settled. The controversy shows the difficulty of trying to read the divine mind.

Interreligious Dialogue

Discussions among Christians and non-Christians take place in different settings and formats.

"Dialogue" indicates an openness and mutuality in sharing perspectives of faith*. Discussions are serious, show respect for dialogue partners, and convey a willingness to learn from others as well as to witness to Christian faith itself. Argumentation and criticism need to be carried out within a greater desire for dialogue and engagements "to seek to bring two religious traditions* together in ways that promote civil society, respect, and—where possible and appropriate—mutual service" (*Engagement*).

Several Reformed theology* perspectives are helpful for considering interreligious dialogue. Reformed theology affirms:

1. God's* freedom* is paramount. God is absolutely free to be God—whatever that will mean. Reformed theology from John Calvin* through Jonathan Edwards through Karl Barth* sees this basic conviction as crucial.
2. Christians confess and proclaim Jesus Christ* as Lord and Savior. Christians are to "be my witnesses" (Acts 1:8) in proclaiming the Gospel of Jesus Christ and announcing "good news of great joy" to all people (Luke 2:10).
3. The Holy Spirit* works more widely than we know. We never know what the Holy Spirit is doing, so we are always open to the work of the Spirit.

These perspectives free Reformed theology and Reformed Christians to be open to dialogue with other religions in a posture of listening and learning. Reliance on the work of the Holy Spirit means Christian witness can be carried out with conviction, and graciously. One listens to learn and perceive ways of the Spirit. Important perspectives from other faiths may turn out to be new avenues of the Spirit. The Spirit may move dialogue partners to wider understandings and even joint actions on issues, situations, or directions where common concerns exist.

Irresistible Grace

In classic Reformed theology*, those whom God* has predestined as the elect to receive the gift of salvation* in Jesus Christ* are "effectually called" to receive God's grace* in Christ. This "effectual call is of God's free and special grace alone, not from anything at all foreseen in man, who is altogether passive therein, until, being quickened and renewed by the Holy Spirit*, he is thereby enabled to answer this call, and to embrace the grace offered and conveyed in it," according to the Westminster Confession* (1647; BC 6.065). The Synod of Dordt (1618–1619) taught God's saving grace is efficacious and effective, overcoming human resistance: "All those in whose hearts God works in this marvelous way are certainly, unfailingly, and effectively reborn and do actually believe" (Dort chs. 3 and 4, art. 12).

This Reformed teaching has been called "Irresistible Grace." Its point is that for Reformed theology, God's grace to the elect is effective not by human efforts but by the work of the Holy Spirit. The Spirit gives faith* and changes the sinful heart, freeing the sinful will so the person may believe in Christ and receive salvation. Or: "God's regenerating grace works powerfully and efficaciously, not coercing a reluctant will by force, but rather spiritually reforming the will to overcome its resistance" (OHRT 248).

Arminian theology taught that God's grace is resistible: Humans may cooperate or effectively resist God's grace. Lutheran theology taught that God's grace comes through means of grace (Scripture*, preaching*); humans may resist grace but not effectively cooperate with God's grace that comes before conversion* (called "prevenient grace").

The Reformed emphasis is on salvation by God's grace—a grace that is not overcome by the sinfulness of humans but that works in God's elect effectively to bring salvation.

J

Justice

Reformed theology* has emphasized justice as a reflection of the character of God* and as God's desire for the ways humans interact with each other, in society and in personal relationships.

John Calvin*, in interpreting Jesus's words about the "greatest commandment" (Matt. 22:34–40) indicated that loving our "neighbor" means loving all, since the Word "applies indiscriminately to any man," for all are neighbors (CNTC 3:37, 38). The Law* and prophets require this love as "the whole foundation and structure of holy, upright living": "service of God and love for men" (3:39). Calvin used the concept of "equity" as a summary of Jesus's Golden Rule (Matt. 7:12). For Calvin, "equity and justice cannot be separated" since "equity is the rule that, when practiced, ensures that all receive justice—what is rightfully theirs" (Equity 51). Not to receive this is "a violation of human justice" (CNTC 8:37). Equity is "the guide that presents such harm" (Equity 51).

Reformed theology sees the Law of God as the guide for believers to indicate how God wants them to live. The Ten Commandments show what love for neighbor should look like. Calvin applied "equity" to love for the needy, saying that each person from their "own abundance should assist the needs of the poor" (CNTC 1:124).

In social justice and corporate ethics, justice is to be practiced in society. Church* members "have to fight against pretensions and injustices when these same powers endanger human welfare. Their strength is in their confidence that God's purpose rather than [human] schemes will finally prevail" (BC 9.25). God's concerns for the poor and those who suffer injustice must be lived out by the church to obey the biblical injunction: "Let justice roll down like water and righteousness like an ever-flowing stream" (Amos 5:24).

Justification

Justification by God's* grace* through faith* is an important Protestant doctrine*. It was central to Martin Luther and importantly clarified and expounded by John Calvin* and later Reformed theology. Calvin called it "the main hinge on which religion turns" (*Inst.* 3.11.1).

Justification is a legal term, used by Paul to speak of the justified person (Rom. 5:1, 9; Gal. 2:16) being a sinner who becomes righteous by the death* of Christ on the cross. Calvin wrote that one is "said to be justified in God's sight who is both reckoned righteous in God's judgment* and has been accepted on account of his righteousness." This is "the remission of sins* and the imputation of Christ's righteousness" (*Inst.* 3.11.2).

Forgiveness* of sin and God's accepting Christ's righteousness as the sinner's own means "imputing the obedience and satisfaction of Christ unto them" (*BC* 6.068). The justified receive the "merits of Christ" applied to them, and they also receive a "union of the believer with Christ by grace through faith" (*DLGTT* 162). Faith is "not merely knowledge and assent. It is also a profound heartfelt or volitional acceptance of Christ that grounds the application of God's grace to believers" (*ERF* 202). An "individual is counted righteous because he is *in Christo*, in Christ, covered as it were by the righteousness of Christ" (*DLGTT* 162). Jesus Christ*, "the Righteous One, indwells the believer" (*OHRT* 506). Forgiveness of sin is still necessary for believers. But forgiveness is given in Christ.

Believers receive a "double grace," said Calvin: reconciliation* with God through Christ's "blamelessness" and a sanctification* by "Christ's spirit" that "we may cultivate blamelessness and purity of life" (*Inst.* 3.11.1). Justification is the gateway to the Christian life in which believers grow in faith and obedience (sanctification), and God's Spirit "dwells in you" (Rom. 8:9, 11; 1 Cor. 3:16).

K

Kingdom of God

A central theme in the preaching* of Jesus was the "kingdom" or "reign" of God*. In the New Testament*, the Kingdom of God is future: "Thy kingdom come" (Matt. 6:10), a theme proclaimed by Old Testament* prophets (Isa. 2:1–5; Zech. 14:9). But Jesus also spoke of the kingdom as present (Mark 1:15; Luke 17:21). Jesus embodied the Kingdom of God, leading early church theologians to speak of the kingdom as (Gr.) autobaselia—a "self-kingdom" in Jesus himself.

Reformed theology* follows these biblical dimensions as it anticipates the ultimate establishment of God's reign and rule over all things at the end of history*, when God will be "all in all" (1 Cor. 15:28; BC 4.123; cf. 7.301), for "the kingdom represents the triumph of God over all that resists [God's] will and disrupts [God's] creation*" (9.54).

The Kingdom of God for the church* and those who are given "a new birth into a living hope* through the resurrection* of Jesus Christ* from the dead" (1 Pet. 1:3) takes practical expression. They live with "an orientation towards the new creation"—living from what is surely coming in the future rather than from what is already within oneself, or the church (Church 278). God's future reign orients and directs the church's mission and ministry* and Christian believers toward a "Messianic Way of Life" (275) in the presence of the Holy Spirit*. This means, too, as Jürgen Moltmann* put it, that Christians are called "to live as strangers in this world" (Coming 310; cf. Heb. 11:13). Christians are "therefore refugees in all the kingdoms of the world" (Coming 310; cf. Heb. 13:14). The "'heavenly Jerusalem' [Heb. 12: 22] becomes for them the symbol of the hoped-for new creation of the world, God's dwelling" (310)—"immediate, omnipresent and eternal" (315).

Knowledge of God

Knowledge of God has been perceived to come in various ways. God's* self-revelation may occur in nature, in Scripture*, and—most significantly—in Jesus Christ*. Reformed theology* has considered these avenues and established understandings of each. Yet the extent and effect of God's self-revelation has been debated among Reformed theologians.

Natural (or general) revelation* refers to a revelation of God in nature. The validity of this means of knowing God has been disputed by Karl Barth*, with Emil Brunner. Is there a valid "natural theology*" whereby God can be known through nature? Brunner accepted a limited possibility here, while Barth, responding in *Nein!* (1934; Eng. trans. 1946), rejected this. Reformed theology does recognize there is a knowledge of God the Creator that can be known once a person has come to know God in Jesus Christ. Thus John Calvin* could speak of God's works in nature as "this most beautiful theater" (*Inst.* 1.14.20).

Scripture is the source of the knowledge of God. Scripture as the "Word of God*" is the means God uses to communicate reliable knowledge of who God is and what God does. The source of the knowledge of God the redeemer—Jesus Christ—is Scripture alone. Those who come to faith* in Jesus Christ do so by the power of the Holy Spirit*, who gives the conviction that Scripture is God's Word and that Jesus Christ is Lord and Savior.

Jesus Christ as the Word of God, the mediator between God and humanity*, and the One who, by his death* on the Cross, provides forgiveness* of sin* is known by "the internal witness" work of the Holy Spirit. The Spirit testifies that "God in person speaks" in Scripture (*Inst.* 1.7.4) and witnesses to who Jesus Christ is. As the incarnate* Son of God, it is in Christ that we know God most clearly.

Knox, John

John Knox (c. 1514–1572) was born in Haddington, Scotland, and became the leading figure in the Scottish Reformation and in Scottish Presbyterianism.

Knox was educated at St. Andrews University and was ordained as a priest. He came under the influence of George Wishart and others and converted to Protestantism. In 1547, he felt God* was calling* him to be a preacher. But Knox and others were captured, and he spent nineteen months as a galley slave. After his release in 1549, Knox went to England, where he was chaplain to the Protestant King Edward VI. With the accession to queen of the Roman Catholic Mary Tudor, Knox went into exile in Europe (January 1554). He met John Calvin* and Heinrich Bullinger* and was pastor for English-speaking congregations in Frankfurt and Geneva. His 1558 work *The First Blast of the Trumpet against the Monstrous Regimen of Women*, against female sovereigns, was against Mary. He wrote other anti–Roman Catholic treatises.

Knox returned to Scotland in May 1559 as a leader of the Reforming Party and a preacher. In 1560, he and others wrote the Scots Confession, which was a strong statement of the emerging Reformed faith*. This was accompanied by a *Book of Discipline*. Knox's *Geneva Service Book* (1542) became a leading resource for Reformed worship*. His vision for a "Christian Commonwealth" as a way to restore the purity of Scottish religion looked to a nation where civil and ecclesiastical powers worked together to establish the "true religion." The Scots Confession said that "the preservation and purification of religion is particularly the duty of kings, princes, rulers, and magistrates," appointed for "civil government* but also to maintain true religion and to suppress all idolatry* and superstition" (BC 3.24).

Knox's influence was long-lasting. His overall contributions to Scottish Presbyterianism were many, especially in worship, theology, and polity*.

L

Law

God's* Law functions in several ways for created persons.

Throughout the Old Testament*, laws were rules for different aspects of life. There were laws for rituals, legal norms, and moral laws to regulate human behavior. The Ten Commandments (Exod. 20) are referred to as the Law of God. These are succinct directions on how humans are to relate to God and how they are to interact with each other.

Martin Luther saw "the law as God's design for human life and therefore often praised it as the Creator's good gift, necessary for instruction of Christians" (OHMLT 172). But the law diagnoses humans as sinners. The law was a mirror to show humans are sinners. The law was a hammer to beat down any thought that humans could justify themselves in the sight of God by their own actions. Relatedly, the law was also a mask for people to look behind and see the Christian Gospel.

John Calvin* also saw the law as a mirror—as it "shows us the spots on our face" (Inst. 2.7.7). The law also can "only accuse, condemn, and destroy." But Calvin's distinctive emphasis—followed also by later Reformed theologians and confessions*—was on the positive function of the law. The law is a good gift of God because it expresses God's will. It functions in a positive way as a guide for Christian believers to know what God desires for their lives. The "proper purpose of the law," wrote Calvin, "finds its place among believers in whose hearts the Spirit of God already lives and reigns," for "here is the best instrument for them to learn more thoroughly each day the nature of the Lord's will to which they aspire, and to confirm them in the understanding of it." The law helps believers to "make fresh progress toward a purer knowledge of the divine will" (2.7.12).

Liberty, Religious

Reformed theology* has developed in a number of places and contexts. Different and emerging theological views have sometimes been influenced more directly by the various settings where Reformed theology was being done.

Religious liberty refers to the opportunity for individuals or groups to express and enact their religious/theological views in a society. This they may do without interference from other powers, such as government* or being subject to penalties levied by the state.

The Reformed tradition* has featured a variety of views about the latitude within which religious beliefs may be expressed without interference. Reformed theology has also pondered whether the church* or the state should decide the limits of societal religious expression and actions.

John Calvin* emphasized the "conscience*" as being the way God* and humans interact (*Inst.* 4.10.3). The conscience of the Christian is "higher than all human judgments" (4.10.5). Since the "magistrate" is "ordained by God" (Rom. 13:1), laws ("good and just laws," wrote Calvin) "made by magistrate or by the church" still "do not of themselves bind the conscience" (*Inst.* 4.10.5). Even "the power of the sword" is "not exercised over consciences" (4.11.8).

Controversies over these points took place during the seventeenth century with the English Revolution and in the struggles within English Puritanism*. In a different context, the Reformed sought to carve out ways of understanding in relation to eighteenth-century developments in the United States.

Whether the church should be ultimately responsible for imposing religious discipline* and worship* has also been a question among the Reformed. A government's suppression of religious liberty has fostered calls for resistance by various means in some places.

A basic guiding principle remains: "God alone is Lord of the conscience." To violate this or act contrary to God's Word* is "to destroy liberty of conscience, and reason* also" (*BC* 6.109).

Liturgy, Reformed

Reformed liturgy is the ordering of the worship* of God*.

Reformed worship seeks to praise and glorify God, and to celebrate God's actions in history*, especially God's grace* in providing salvation* in Jesus Christ*. Worship is the worship of the triune God as Creator, Sustainer, and Redeemer. Public worship and its liturgy reflect the story of salvation.

While the "order" of the liturgy varies among churches, Reformed liturgies feature rubrics that reflect Reformed theological understandings. These include:

1. Gathering. The community hears a Call to Worship (Scripture* verse); Hymn of Praise; Confession and Forgiveness*—A unison Prayer* of Confession of Sins*; Declaration of Pardon; Hymn of Praise
2. Word and Sacrament. The community hears the Word of God*; Prayer for Illumination; Reading of Scripture; Proclamation of God's Word in a Sermon; Hymn; Affirmation of Faith*; Baptism*; Prayers of Intercession; Lord's Supper*; Offering
3. Sending. Closing Hymn or other Acts of Commitment; Blessing and Charge to the People; Service in the World

The frequency of the celebration of the Lord's Supper has varied within Reformed churches. John Calvin* believed "no meeting of the church* should take place without the Word, prayers, partaking of the Supper, and almsgiving" (*Inst.* 4.17.44). But while Calvin preferred weekly celebrations of the Supper, he was overruled by the Geneva city government. So he had the Supper celebrations rotated among the Genevan churches so the Supper was celebrated weekly in some church. In Scotland, the quarterly celebration of the Supper became the norm; a practice that carried over to Presbyterian churches in the United States until the 1960s, when more frequent Supper celebrations became more standard.

Preaching* and prayers* express hearing the Word of God in believing human words can convey God's Word when spoken and applied to hearers. In prayer, the congregation brings all things before God.

Lord's Supper

With baptism*, the Lord's Supper is one of the two sacraments* of Reformed churches. It is also called the Eucharist* or Communion. It was instituted by Jesus on the eve of his crucifixion in a common meal celebrated with his disciples.

The Supper is "an abundant feast of theological meaning." It includes "thanksgiving to God* the Father; remembrance of Jesus Christ*; invocation of the Holy Spirit*; communion in the body of Christ; and a meal of the realm of God" (DW 3.0409). The Supper is a sign of God's covenant*, spoken by Jesus: "This cup is the new covenant in my blood. Do this, as often as you drink it, in remembrance of me" (1 Cor. 11:25).

The Supper is linked with the bread of Passover and with the manna in the wilderness. The Supper is a sacrament of praise*, a sign of thanksgiving for God's steadfast love. The Supper also reflects God's calling* to feed others as believers have been fed. The Supper anticipates the heavenly banquet of God, when tears end and death* is eternally vanquished.

Further, "the Lord's Supper enacts and seals what the Word proclaims: God's sustaining grace* offered to all people. The Lord's Supper is at once God's gift of grace, God's means of grace, and God's call to respond to that grace. Through the Lord's Supper, Jesus Christ nourishes us in righteousness, faithfulness, and discipleship. Through the Lord's Supper, the Holy Spirit renews the Church* in its identity and sends the Church to mission in the world" (DW 3.0409).

The Supper is God's accommodation* to human weakness through which God's promises of salvation* in Jesus Christ are sealed for believers (Inst. 4.17). Christ is genuinely present in the Supper—but not locally or physically present. The Supper is a "visible word of God*" (a term of Augustine's that John Calvin* cited in Inst. 4.14.6).

M

Millennialism

Millennialism is a set of beliefs based on the "thousand years" of Christ's reign, as mentioned in Rev. 20:2–7. Millennialism has developed as a form of Christian eschatology*. Millennialism is also called "chiliasm" (Gr. *chilioi*: "thousand"). Three main interpretations have emerged.

Premillennialism teaches that Christ's second coming can be anticipated when certain "signs of the times" occur: natural catastrophes, apostasy, the emergence of the Antichrist, and a great tribulation for the people of God*. Christ will return to earth before the millennium begins. Variations of this view were held by early church* theologians including Irenaeus, Justin Martyr, and Tertullian.

Postmillennialism teaches that Christ's second coming will come after the success of the Gospel and righteousness, by God's grace*, which will be a millennial period. Jonathan Edwards was a proponent of this view.

Amillennialism has been the viewpoint of a number of Reformed theologians. They emphasize God's kingdom* being at work throughout history*, coexisting with the kingdom of evil. This is the period of the "church militant" or the church on earth. This period continues until the end of history. Amillennialism does not interpret the "thousand years" image literally; instead, the image represents the whole historical period between the resurrection* of Jesus Christ* and his return to earth ("Second Coming"). Augustine, John Calvin* and many Reformed confessions* hold this view.

In what may be a too-unrefined description, some have said these three streams of millennialism evoke particular emphases. Premillennialism stresses evangelism* in anticipation of the return of Christ and the coming millennium. Postmillennialism stresses social action and the creation of better societies featuring justice* and peace*. Amillennialism can combine both the other emphases—not for the sake of when a "millennium" may come but as a basic matter of faithfulness to the Christian Gospel.

A light comment is one who said: "I'm *pro-mil*"; I am "pro" the millennium—whenever it happens!

Ministry

Those who serve God* in Jesus Christ* in the church* and the world engage in ministry. The calling* to minister is by God's Holy Spirit* to the whole people of God, the church. Some ministries are recognized by the church as ongoing forms, such as ministries of pastors, preachers, missionaries, and the like. But the ministries of Christians in the church are varied—from highly visible to nearly "invisible"—since they consist of one-to-one service to one another in the name of Jesus Christ.

Jesus himself is the chief "minister," as he said: "I am among you as one who serves" (Luke 22:27; Gr. *diakonia*: "service"; Lat. *minister*: "servant"). Many Reformed churches have the formal office of deacon*, in which the needs of the community are met, an office emphasized by John Calvin* in Geneva. More broadly, church offices are for "the exercise of the ministry entrusted to and enjoined upon the whole congregation" (BC 8.25), for "each member is the church in the world, endowed by the Spirit with some gift of ministry and is responsible for the integrity of his witness in his own particular situation" (9.38; Eph. 4:12). All Christians are called (vocation*) to live as Christ's disciples. Jesus's service to others "commits the church to work for every form of human well-being" (BC 9.32).

Reformed churches recognize the church offices: elders*, deacons, pastors, and teachers. Ministries of the church are continuously carried out through these ministries of leadership and oversight: worship*, preaching*, teaching, service to others through expressions of love and caregiving. Corporate ministries of the church may be seen through the lens of reconciliation*, since "to be reconciled to God is to be sent into the world as his reconciling community" (BC 9.31). The Holy Spirit guides the church and Christ's disciples into new forms of service and ministries.

Moltmann, Jürgen

Jürgen Moltmann (b. 1926) is an important Reformed theologian who is well known for his "theology of hope*."

Moltmann became a prisoner of war in England (1945–1947) while in the German army. In 1948, he began to study theology at the University of Göttingen and was influenced by Karl Barth*. Moltmann's own theology developed, especially as he focused on eschatology*. He spent his career teaching at Tübingen, where he gained worldwide recognition.

Moltmann's work is rooted in John Calvin's* eschatological emphases, including God's* providence* and his ethical convictions about the Lordship of Jesus Christ*. Moltmann wrote that "Christian faith* is essentially faith in the resurrection*. Faith in the resurrection means being born again to hope" (*Experiences* 31; cf. *TOH* 194). Hope is "a command. Obeying it means life, survival, endurance, standing up to life until death* is swallowed up in victory. Obeying it means never giving way to the forces of annihilation in resignation or rage" (*Experiences* 20). This means active engagement in life for all who follow "the way of Jesus Christ" in suffering solidarity with the world (*Way* 180–81). Hope recognizes in Christ's resurrection "the future of God for the world" (*TOH* 194). The church* in the power of the Spirit is "engaged in the apostolate of hope for the world and finds therein its essence." The church is "not the salvation* of the world," but "it serves the coming salvation of the world and is like an arrow sent out into the world to point to the future" (328).

Moltmann has a full trinitarian theology. He wrote about the "rebirth of the whole creation": "Fellowship with the crucified Jesus leads to the fellowship of the world's messianic suffering. Fellowship with the risen Christ leads to the dawn of the liberty of the messianic era" (*Church* 288).

~

N

Natural Theology

Attempts to know God* by the use of reason* or experience, apart from revelation* that comes from God in a special form ("special revelation") constitute natural theology.

Thomas Aquinas distinguished "natural" theology from "revealed" theology. Aquinas developed five "theistic proofs" for God's existence. The Roman Catholic church* taught that "God may certainly be known by the natural light of human reason, by means of created things" (Vatican I, 1870; cited in I. John Hesselink, "Natural Theology," in ERF 251). This "natural theology" could not penetrate the divine mysteries and so needed to be supplemented by knowledge from God's special revelation.

Reformed theologians have referred to natural theology, but this is as a prologue to revealed theology. John Calvin* devoted book I of his Institutes to the Knowledge of God* the Creator. He believed in a "sense of divinity*" (Lat. sensus divinitatis), which was a "seed of religion" that formed an innate knowledge of God's existence in all people (Inst. 1.3.1, 3; 4.1).

But due to human sin*, this knowledge is "smothered" or "corrupted" (Inst. 1.4). This means humans are responsible for not knowing God (due to Adam's fall into sin; 1.2.1). Whatever recognitions one might have of God in nature, when it comes to salvation*, "the greatest geniuses are blinder than moles!" (2.2.18).

Emil Brunner and Karl Barth* debated this issue. Brunner believed in a natural theology or general revelation that could be seen in the "orders of creation*," including God's image in humanity*. Barth replied sharply in Nein! (1934; Eng. trans. 1946): God is known only in Jesus Christ*. Barth's view is in the Theological Declaration of Barmen*: "Jesus Christ, as he is attested for us in Holy Scripture*, is the one Word of God* which we have to hear and which we have to trust and obey in life and in death*" (BC 8.11).

For the Reformed, no form of natural theology in itself can bring the knowledge of salvation.

Neo-Orthodoxy

Neo-Orthodoxy, also called "Dialectical theology," refers to the theologies of twentieth-century Reformed theologians, including Karl Barth* and Emil Brunner; in America, Reinhold Niebuhr; and in Scotland, Donald and John Baillie and others. The term was coined by critics who saw these theological approaches as trying to reinvigorate or revise traditional "orthodox" Christian theology. For critics, the "old orthodoxy" should be jettisoned more completely. But for "Neo-Orthodox" theologians—in light of World War I, especially—theology needed renewal in continuity with Reformation theology, including its emphasis on the witness of the "Word of God*"—in Jesus Christ* and Scripture*—which tells the truth that the world cannot redeem or save itself. Only God* can break in and break through with the message of salvation* and reconciliation* in Jesus Christ.

God is "wholly other" from humanity*. Human sin* creates a great gulf between creature and Creator, a distance to be overcome only by God's act of self-revelation in Jesus Christ. God in Christ is humanity's judge but also its redeemer. Jesus was crucified, but risen—hidden, yet revealed. Jesus Christ speaks "No" and "Yes" to humanity. Divine revelation* is the source of the true knowledge of God*. There is no human continuity—of reason*, ethics, or religious experience—between humans and God's self-revelation in Jesus Christ. Through his death* on the cross, Christ is the sole means of reconciliation: "Jesus Christ is the atonement*" (CD IV/1, 34). Christ established victory over the power of sin. God's forgiveness* in Christ is the only means to true freedom* and to the redeemed life of faith* in which humans become a "new creation" (2 Cor. 5:17) who have "escaped from death and partakes of life" (Knowledge 81).

Neo-Orthodoxy critiqued liberal theology, but it has been suggested that Barth's theology and Gustavo Gutiérrez's liberation theology have some "mutually reinforcing convictions" (HKBCMM 99).

New Testament

The early Christian church* received the Jewish Scriptures*. It also received the words of Jesus, handed down initially by oral traditions* and then as written Gospels. Letters of the apostles circulated indicating the importance of the person and work of Jesus for believers in churches. The book of Acts and the Revelation of John also became documents through which the church heard apostolic teachings. The church settled on the twenty-seven books of the New Testament as its canon or list of sacred books. These were received as "the spiritual and therefore complete and authentic fulfillment of the Old Testament*" (RD 4:660). With the Old Testament, the New Testament is considered in Reformed theology* as having been given "by inspiration of God*, to be the rule of faith* and life" (BC 6.002).

Most generally, Reformed theology has recognized "the Old and New Testaments are reducible to these two primary heads. The Old promises Christ to come and the New testifies that he has come" (Marrow 202). As Jesus said, "The Law* and the Prophets were until John came; since then the good news of the kingdom of God* is being proclaimed" (Luke 16:16).

Jesus as God's promised Messiah provides salvation* through his death* and resurrection* (John 3:16) to all who believe—Jew and Gentile. In Christ, the "dividing wall of hostility" between peoples is broken down (Eph. 2:11–22); sin* is forgiven (Rom. 3:25; 5:1–11); and reconciliation of humanity* with God is made real (2 Cor. 5:16–21). As Herman Bavinck wrote: "The benefits of salvation promised and foreshadowed under the Old Testament have become manifest in Christ as eternal and authentic reality. . . . The Old Testament was not abolished but fulfilled in the new dispensation, is still consistently being fulfilled, and will be fulfilled, until the Parousia of Christ" (RD 4:661).

8

Offices of Christ

In Reformed theology*, the threefold office (Lat. *munus triplex*) of Jesus Christ* has been seen as Christ being Prophet, Priest, and King. This formulation was emphasized by John Calvin*. Martin Luther had spoken of Christ as priest and king. Calvin developed the typology more fully (*Inst.* 2.15), and his discussion became most significant for Reformed theology. The threefold office is explicated in the Heidelberg Catechism (1563; BC 4.031) and the Westminster Confession* (1647; BC 6.043).

Christ's "office" in Reformed theology is the office of mediator. It is through Christ and Christ alone that salvation* is accomplished. As William Ames noted, "The office itself to which Christ is called is threefold; namely, that of prophet, priest, and king." This order, said Ames, corresponds with the order in which salvation is brought, obtained, and applied (*Marrow* 132).

Christ as Prophet, said Calvin, is the one who brought "perfect doctrine*." In Christ's teachings, "all parts of perfect wisdom are contained," for "outside Christ, there is nothing worth knowing" (*Inst.* 2.15.2).

Christ as Priest is our everlasting intercessor who "as a pure and stainless Mediator he is by his holiness to reconcile us to God*." Now, believers have "trust in prayer* but also peace* for godly consciences" (*Inst.* 2.15.6).

Christ as King rules spiritually over the church* and all its adversaries. Despite our personal lots in life, we are content that "our King will never leave us destitute, but will provide for our needs until, our warfare ended, we are called to triumph." Christ "fulfills the combined duties of king and pastor for the godly who submit willingly and obediently" (*Inst.* 2.15.5).

Reformed theology recognizes Christ's mediatorial office is eternal. This belongs to Christ as the preexistent Word during the Old Testament* period to his being the Word incarnate* during both his earthly work and his eternal reign.

Old Testament

Reformed theology* accepts the canon of the Old Testament as the thirty-nine books of the Hebrew Bible. The "Apocrypha," rising from the Septuagint (Greek translation), are books not in the Hebrew Scriptures* and not considered as inspired by God*. They are not accepted as canonical by Protestants, including the Reformed (BC 6.003; cf. 6.008).

The Old Testament is divided into three parts: Torah (Law*)—the five "books of Moses"; Prophets (Heb. Nebiim)—Former and Latter Prophets; and the Writings (Heb. Kethubim). The whole Old Testament is considered sacred Scripture, God's revelation* to the Patriarchs and to Israel as God's covenant* people. Reformed theologians speak of the Old Testament as the "Old Covenant," which anticipates the "New Covenant," the New Testament*, centered in God's Messiah, Jesus Christ*.

The Reformed emphasize that the Old Covenant, constituted by the various covenants of the Old Testament, is the "same" in "substance and reality" as the New Covenant—"yet they differ in the mode of dispensation," said John Calvin* (Inst. 2.10.2). This covenantal structure of Scripture led to emphasizing the "similarity of the Old and New Testaments" as well as the "difference between the Two Testaments" (2.10; 2.11). Chiefly, "the Old Testament is revealed in the New, while the New Testament is concealed in the Old" (RD 4:661).

Theologically, God's purposes for salvation* and establishing a "people of God" are at work throughout the Old Testament. Faith* was the means of living in relationship with God, as exemplified by Abraham as "the best model of believing" (Inst. 2.10.11). He and other members of God's covenant people received a "promise of spiritual and eternal life" (2.10.23), for "the Old Testament always had its end in Christ and in eternal life" (2.10.4). All this is by God's grace*, the "free mercy of God" (2.10.4), through God's promises to be God to God's people (Lev. 26:12; Inst. 2.10.8).

In the Old Testament, God's people knew that "however the saints were buffeted about, their final end was to be life and salvation" (Inst. 2.10.18).

Ordination

Reformed theology* recognizes ordination as an act of the church* where persons who are called to various specific ministries* are "set apart" to be recognized for these forms of service.

Ordination is an act of the church. In Reformed churches with Presbyterian polity*, ordination to the ministry* of Word and Sacrament is an act of a presbytery* or classis. Ordination is administered by the church to the person and under the consent of the governing body where the ministry to which ordination is being bestowed. Ordination is to a recognized, validated ministry, and the person to be ordained has obtained the requisite affirmative vote of the ordaining body for this ordination. Ordination to special ministries is also carried out by the governing body.

In local congregations, elders* and deacons* are ordained. This ordination takes place after a vote of the congregation, electing lay persons to these ministries.

Ordinations are carried out in the context of public worship* for both actions of governing bodies and local congregations. Ordination is marked by the "laying on of hands" (1 Tim. 4:14). This feature is a public recognition of the role of the larger church. It also points to the continuity of Christian ministries with the historic church by use of this biblical action. The prayers that attend ordination services are invocations of the Holy Spirit* for the ongoing power and grace* to support and bless the ministries ordination anticipates.

In all ordinations, there is the recognition that "we have gifts that differ according to the grace given to us" (Rom. 12:6). This is why, in addition to the ongoing ministries of the church, ordination can be to specialized ministries. Notably, Fred Rogers ("Mr. Rogers") was ordained by Pittsburgh Presbytery in 1963 for the specialized ministry to "do his ministry with children and their families through the mass media."

Original Sin

Original sin is a theological understanding, prominent in Reformed theology*, that indicates humanity* is sinful in its "origins" as humans. The Genesis story of Adam and Eve indicates the first sin*, or transgression against God*, which led to the couple's banishment from the Garden of Eden. From that story, the theological recognition came that sin is a mark of humanity, so humans are born in sin, and that sin has drastic effects in the lives of humans in relation to God. As the Psalmist indicated, "I was born guilty, a sinner when my mother conceived me" (Ps. 51:5). The universal effect of sin is indicated by Paul: "All have sinned and fall short of the glory of God" (Rom. 3:23), and the results of sin are also shown: "The wages of sin is death*" (Rom. 6:23).

The inherited effects of sin are mentioned in the Scots Confession (1560): "By this transgression, generally known as original sin, the image of God* was utterly defaced in man, and he and his children became by nature hostile to God, slaves to Satan, and servants to sin" (BC 3.03). Humans are guilty before God and alienated from their Creator. Actual sins follow from sinful human nature. The far-reaching effects of sin include the loss of "free will*" and any ability by humans to forgive their own sin or to establish a relationship of love and trust with God. Thus, humanity "hath wholly lost all ability of will to any spiritual good accompanying salvation*" (6.061; cf. 5.043–45).

Humanity's imputed guilt for sin can be removed only by the work of the "Second Adam," Jesus Christ*. Said Paul: "Therefore just as one man's trespass led to condemnation for all, so one man's act of righteousness leads to justification* and life for all" (Rom. 5:18).

Orthodoxy, Reformed

Reformed Orthodoxy refers to "the period of institutionalization and codification following the Reformation. Beginning in the late sixteenth century and extending into the eighteenth century, it would be the dominant form of Reformed theology* for nearly two hundred years" (CRO 11; cf. ERF 265–69).

"Orthodoxy" is understood as "the process and period in which the theology of the Reformers was systematized, summarized, and elaborated upon in theological handbooks, confessions*, tracts, sermons, and so forth" (CRO 2). Academic assistance for teaching the emerging Reformed Orthodoxy at new Reformed academies and universities came from the "scholastic method." Scholasticism was a hallmark of medieval philosophy and theology, drawing from the work of Thomas Aquinas. Reformed Orthodox theologians used the method, which features the "*quaestio* technique characterized by presenting a thesis or a thematic question, followed by the treatment of objections against the adopted positions (*objectiones*)" (15).

Four phases of Reformed Orthodoxy are early orthodoxy (1565–1620), high orthodoxy (1620–1700), a transitional phase influenced by pietism (1700–1740), and late orthodoxy (1740–1800). Parallel to Reformed Orthodoxy were similar periods of Lutheran Orthodoxy in which the theologies of Martin Luther and his colleagues were developed further using scholastic methods. Orthodox Lutheran and Reformed theologians were open to the use of reason* and philosophy, "specifically to the revised Aristotelianism of the late Renaissance" (ERF 265).

Some have seen Reformed Orthodoxy as a "fatal deviation from the Reformation" (CRO 12). Scholasticism is considered a perversion of John Calvin's* theology in this "negative continuity theory." A "positive continuity theory" seeks to examine the Reformed scholastics on their own terms, in their own theological contexts, so values of their work are not tied to exact replications of Calvin's thought (14).

Important Reformed Orthodox theologians include Theodore Beza, Zacharias Ursinus, Caspar Olevianus, Girolamo Zanchi, Franciscus Junius, Amandus Polanus, Franciscus Gomarus, Johannes Maccovius, Johannes the Elder and Johannes the Younger Buxtorf, Francis Turretin, and Johann Heinrich Heidegger.

P

Pastoral Care

Pastoral care in Reformed understanding is a structured ministry* that provides a "means of grace*" to those in need. This ministry takes shape formally, as in a pastor/parishioner relationship, or informally as Christians in the church* express care and Christian love for one another.

Pastoral care is concerned with the whole of life. Traditional areas in the church where pastoral care takes shape include pastoral visits to church members, comfort for the sick and grieving, and meeting various needs from physical assistance and needs for the necessities of life as well as providing for psychological or spiritual assistance. Forgiveness* for those experiencing guilt and the overall "cure of souls" are dimensions of pastoral care exercised by clergy and the church as the fellowship of faith*.

For Reformed theology*, pastoral care realizes that God* in Jesus Christ* is in the midst of all life. All needs and cares can be brought into dialogue and cast upon Christ, who is the "primary pastor" for believers, the "Good Shepherd" (John 10:11, 14). As Reformed pastor Eduard Thurneysen wrote, "Pastoral care claims to see even the remotest human concerns in their relationship to God, established by Jesus Christ" (*Pastoral* 118).

Care for others can be rendered in different ways by many people. The church's care is rooted and grounded in theological understandings (*see* "Pastoral Theology") and specifically the conviction that Jesus Christ is "the Word made flesh" (John 1:14) who enters the whole of human life. Jesus commanded his disciples to "love one another" (John 13:34; 15:12). Thus, whatever is "human" is of concern to Jesus, and Jesus commands us to love, as he loved, in care. For the Reformed, pastoral care has the "purpose of maintaining an awareness of God's presence and activity in the world and interpreting that presence in people's lives" (*ERF* 271).

Pastoral Theology

Pastoral theology is the theological understanding of ways in which the Word of God* relates to human life and experience through the work* of ministry*. This involves a theology of the whole human being in all aspects of existence.

Pastoral theology in Reformed understanding is grounded in who humans are before God*—as created, as fallen into sin*, and as made "new creations" (2 Cor. 5:17) in Jesus Christ*. These understandings make the concerns and care of persons primary to the pastoral theologian. Understandings of oneself become the point at which pastoral theology and a person can become engaged.

Pastoral theology attempts to provide biblical/theological insights for the work of ministry as care is exercised to those in need. Perceptions of persons' self-understandings and needs are helped to be formed by theological understandings. These understandings can span across a variety of dimensions of human life: family, sexuality, illness, death*, and other elements.

Pastoral theology exercised in the context of pastoral ministries in churches addresses issues of need in light of the church's theological understandings. These include issues of the need for faith*, forgiveness*, repentance*, reconciliation*, moral and ethical* actions, and other dimensions of Christian faith, in Reformed understandings.

A goal in Pastoral theology is for persons to receive new life in Christ and to experience the wholeness of salvation* and growth in faith. The conviction of Pastoral theology as the truth of the Gospel is expressed, as John Calvin* said, when "the sinner does not dwell upon his own compunction or tears, but fixes both eyes upon the Lord's mercy alone" (Inst. 3.4.3). In and through all the weariness, challenges, and difficulties of life, a person is called upon "to seek refreshment, rest, and freedom*" and in "humility to give glory to God" (3.4.3).

Peace

Peace is an important biblical concept. The Hebrew term for peace, *shalom*, means wholeness, harmony, and right relations. It is a very concrete term to describe relationships among nations and people.

Peace in the New Testament* is marked by "peace with God*," which means an end to the hostility that human sin* evinces against God. Jesus Christ* is "peace," who, through his death*, brings reconciliation and peace with God: "Since we are justified by faith*, we have peace with God through our Lord Jesus Christ," wrote Paul (Rom. 5:1). The "new humanity*" in Christ means hostilities between peoples and nations are abolished (Eph. 2:15–17). Christians practice a "ministry* of reconciliation" in this world (2 Cor. 5:12–18).

Human efforts for peace come from the God who desires peace, not violence, and has established this peace and reconciliation in Jesus Christ (Col. 1:20). Christians work* for "justice*, freedom*, and peace" and are "emissaries of peace" (BC 11.4; 9.25). Karl Barth* wrote, "The ministry of reconciliation also commits us to work honestly and earnestly for peace among the nations. In view of the means of mass destruction, war is less than ever a possible solution of political and ideological tension between nations and power blocks" (*Fragments* 58).

Since World War II, Reformed theology*—and churches—have put an emphasis of "peace" as a central dimension of the Gospel of Jesus Christ. It is a ministry that is very much "the believers' calling*." For "peacemaking, is the calling of the Christian church*, for Christ is our peace who has made us one through his body on the cross" and "those who follow our Lord have a special calling as peacemakers" (*Peacemaking* 6).

Reformed theology emphasizes the crucial role peace—grounded in Christ—plays in salvation* and reconciliation—of humans with God and with each other.

Perseverance of the Saints

The "perseverance of the saints" is a testimony to the "perseverance of God* with the saints." The God who elects persons for salvation* is the God who maintains their lives to eternal salvation. Those God regenerates* and brings to faith* will not fall back ("backslide") into sin* to lose the salvation given them in Jesus Christ* by the power of the Holy Spirit*. The power of God keeps them in the bonds of faith until the end. This faithfulness of God was announced by Jesus: "I give them eternal life, and they will never perish. No one will snatch them out of my hand" (John 10:28). Another way to put it is to say those who are held in the hands of God will not slip through God's fingers!

This Reformed emphasis was expressed at the Synod of Dordt (the Fifth Main Point of the Doctrine), in the Westminster Confession* (1647), and in other Reformed confessional writings. Reformed theology* recognizes that believers experience temptation and still sin after justification*, but they will never fall beyond God's grace* and are eternally upheld by God's power. Lapses in the exercise of faith will only be temporary. Persons do not persevere by their own strength but by God's graciousness. They do not forfeit faith or God's grace. This view was counter to Arminian teachings. Lutherans believe there is the possibility of loss of faith due to sin.

The Westminster Confession explains the theological basis for perseverance. Perseverance depends "not upon their own free-will, but upon the immutability of the decree of election*, flowing from the free and unchangeable love of God the Father; upon the efficacy of the merit and intercession of Jesus Christ; the abiding of the Spirit and of the seed of God within them; and the nature of the covenant* of grace" (BC 6.095).

Piety

John Calvin* provided a classic definition of piety: "I call 'piety' that reverence joined with love of God* which the knowledge of his benefits induces" (Inst. 1.2.1). Reverence and love combine to form true pietas. In classical Latin, this term referred to the relationship of children to their parents. Children were to fear, honor, obey, and love their parents. As Ford Lewis Battles wrote, "Pietas bespoke the mutual love and care between parents and their offspring" (Piety 15).

A measure of the Christian's reverence and love for God in Christ is captured by the Heidelberg Catechism's: "What is your only comfort in life and in death*?" with its Answer: "That I am not my own, but belong—body and soul, in life and in death—to my faithful Savior, Jesus Christ*" (BC 4.001). Believers belong fully to their Savior, Jesus Christ—in life and death. This is assurance of the deepest possible relationship between "child" and "parent." The "pious mind," said Calvin, acknowledges God as "Lord and Father" and will "observe his authority* in all things, reverence his majesty, take care to advance his glory, and obey his commandments" (Inst. 1.2.2).

Reformed piety as a way of Christian life takes place in sanctification*, as believers grow in faith*. Piety is a full life of devotion to God, living in the church* and its worship*, studying Scripture*, living in prayer*, participating in sacraments*. Reformed piety engages fully and vigorously in the community and the world, grounded in theological understandings of the God who loves in Jesus Christ and guides by the Holy Spirit*. Piety will pursue peace* and justice*, seek to meet the needs of others, participate in efforts for the good of society, and share love. In short: one will "do everything for the glory of God" (1 Cor. 10:31).

Politics

Politics is the process where people in communities choose leaders and decide how to use resources they hold in common.

Reformed theology* acknowledges the place politics has in the lives of the people of God*. With an emphasis on serving God in this world, Reformed theology realizes the importance of Christians being engaged in political processes, seeking the best for their societies—in line with the will and purposes of God. The Confession of 1967 says, "The members of the church* are emissaries of peace* and seek the good of man in cooperation with powers and authorities in politics, culture, and economics*" (BC 9.25). Sanctification* in the Christian life engages not only one's devotion to God but also the use of one's life—and the church's life—for the good of others. This entails engaging in and cooperating with political processes. Reformed Christians have taken leadership roles in cultures, participating in politics intending to enhance the lives of those they serve in accord with theological and ethical perspectives valued by the Reformed faith*.

The Confession goes on to say, however: "But they have to fight against pretensions and injustices when these same powers endanger human welfare. Their strength is in their confidence that God's purpose rather than man's schemes will finally prevail" (BC 9.25). Power in politics can be wielded for good or evil. With a strong doctrine* of sin*, Reformed theology recognizes the "fallen nature" of systems and processes and the dangers to human welfare that can occur when bad politics has entrenched power. Evils emerge and the lives of citizens can be endangered. Oppression, injustice, wars, and other harms can be the tone and tenor of politics.

Reformed Christians put hope* in God as they work* in politics to stand against evil and to enact God's purposes.

Polity

Polity refers to church* government. Historically, there have been three types of church government. Episcopal polity is led by bishops. Congregational polity is carried out by church congregations in which church members make decisions. Presbyterian polity is led by leaders chosen by the congregation, typically called elders*.

Reformed theology* has functioned within all three types of church polity. Presbyterian and Congregational forms of government have been dominant for Reformed churches, reflecting Reformed theology; however, some Reformed churches have provided for bishops.

Reformed polity in its Presbyterian expression has sought to be scriptural, committed to recognizing Jesus Christ* as Lord of the church and the church as the "body of Christ" (1 Cor. 12). Decision-making is corporate. Decisions about the church's beliefs and life of ministry* are made by governing bodies, led by "moderators," and composed of a parity of ministers of Word and Sacrament and elders who govern together.

Local churches are governed by the session. It is moderated by the minister and composed of elders elected by the congregation. All ministers belong to the presbytery* that encompasses churches in a particular area. The presbytery oversees ministers, sessions, and congregation. The presbytery ordains all ministers of Word and Sacrament. The General Assembly* is the highest body.

Reformed churches are governed by church constitutions. In the Presbyterian Church (USA), the *Book of Confessions* indicates the denomination's theological beliefs. The *Book of Order* is composed of the Form of Government and Directory for Worship, indicating how the church makes decisions and worships. The Rules of Discipline convey procedures for discipline* and the church's judicial processes, aimed toward redemption and mercy.

A traditional motto is: "The church reformed and always being reformed according to the Word of God*." This applies to church beliefs and also its polity.

Prayer

The Westminster Larger Catechism (1648) asks: "What is prayer?" It answers: "Prayer is an offering up of our desires unto God*, in the name of Christ, by the help of his Spirit, with confession of our sins, and thankful acknowledgment of his mercies" (BC 7.288).

John Calvin* defined prayer as "conversation with God" (Inst. 3.20.4); indeed, also "intimate conversation" (3.20.5). In prayer, believers make their requests known to God (Phil. 4: 6), in the name of Christ (the Westminster Shorter Catechism says, "for things agreeable to his will" [BC 7.098]), with the help of the Holy Spirit*, "our teacher in prayer" (Inst. 3.20.5). Believers ask for God to forgive their sins* while they also acknowledge God's many mercies to them. Prayer is an act that involves the one who prays, plus the whole Trinity*: Father, Son, and Holy Spirit.

Throughout Reformed theology*, attention is given to prayer. Prayer is called "the chief exercise of faith*" by Calvin (Inst. 3.20). Prayer enables believers to join with the Spirit of God and be led by the Spirit. Prayer connects believers with the purposes of God, the sovereign, loving Lord who desires believers to pray in trust, as Jesus said. Prayers are made in the "name" of Jesus. This expresses the conviction that Jesus continually makes "intercession" for believers with God (Heb. 7:25). Believers pray for themselves, for the church*, and for others.

God's answers to prayers can come in many ways. Faith recognizes God's answers as God works through various means to accomplish the divine purposes. God's answers to prayer may come quickly or may not become apparent for a long period of time. Continuing prayers may be part of God's answers to one's prayers. While God's means of answering may not be clear, faith in God's love means God is actively at work.

Preaching

"The Preaching of the Word of God* is the Word of God," proclaimed Heinrich Bullinger* in the Second Helvetic Confession (1566; BC 5.004). This expressed the commitment of Reformed theologians since the sixteenth century that in the human act of preaching, God's* Word—God's very self—is proclaimed.

Karl Barth* emphasized the threefold form of the Word of God: Jesus Christ*, Scripture*, and Proclamation. God's revelation* of the divine self comes through this threefold form. For Barth, in preaching "we have to do with the Word of God in an undiminished meaning of the term and therefore with God Himself" (CD I/2, 745).

Preaching is based on proclaiming the message of Holy Scripture and its central focus: Jesus Christ as God's Son and reconciler of the world (2 Cor. 5:16–21). In preaching, God speaks through human preachers—God's "ambassadors"—that, as John Calvin* said, "through their mouths [God] may do his own work—just as a workman uses a tool to do his work*" (Inst. 4.3.1). God uses human preachers to communicate God's Word and will to hearers. So "preaching is the 'Word of God' in that it participates in God's purpose, is initiated by Christ, and is supported by the Spirit with community in the world" (Homiletic 456).

A Reformed (and Protestant) emphasis is that Word and Spirit are inextricably linked together. The Holy Spirit* makes preaching "become" the "Word of God" to hearers. In the church* community, the Spirit works to create new life, new people, new situations, a "new creation." The Spirit energizes the Word as the Word proclaims the work of God's Spirit in the world and supremely in the revelation and act of God's reconciling work in Jesus Christ. The sermon is "the word of God that presents Jesus Christ in the worship* service by the power of the Holy Spirit" (Profound 71).

Predestination

God's* choosing of some persons to receive the gift of salvation* in Jesus Christ* is called election* or predestination.

Augustine developed the doctrine* in *On the Predestination of the Saints*, and it was important to John Calvin*, who wrote that predestination is "God's eternal decree*, by which he compacted with himself what he willed to become of each man" (*Inst.* 3.21.5). In life, the elect receive the "call" of God and the gift of faith* in Jesus Christ; justification* for the forgiveness* of sins*, establishing a right relationship with God; and after death*, entrance into glory, "in which the fulfillment of that election lies" (3.21.7).

Predestination is an act of God's grace*, since salvation is not merited by any creature. Undeserving sinners, whose will is in bondage to the power of sin, cannot choose to receive reconciliation by themselves. They must receive the gift of the Holy Spirit* to become a "new creation" (2 Cor. 5:17; regeneration*) and receive faith for salvation.

In his *Institutes*, Calvin's discussion of predestination was in the context of "The Way We Receive the Grace of Christ" (book III). Here he spoke of election being in Jesus Christ (Eph. 1:4) who is "the mirror wherein we must, and without self-deception may, contemplate our own election" (*Inst.* 3.24.5). This is a doctrine* of comfort. If one believes in Christ, this is a sign of election.

Later Reformed theologians treated predestination in relation to the order of God's divine decrees*. The decree of predestination was divided into election* (Lat. *election*) and reprobation* (*reprobation*), the latter being those whom God leaves within their sin or passes over to face eternal punishment (*DLGTT* 234–35, 263).

Karl Barth* saw election as the "sum of the gospel" (*CD* II/2, 12) and taught that Christ was the subject of double predestination as both elect and reprobate, in whom all humanity is elect (*OXRT* 143; *CD* II/2, §33).

122   Reformed Theology from A to Z

Priesthood of Believers

Martin Luther emphasized that the church* is a "royal priesthood" (1 Pet. 2:9–10; Rev. 1:6; 5:10) in which all believers share in a common priesthood. The church is in and with Jesus Christ*, who is the only true "high priest" (Heb. 3:1).

Reformed understandings agree with this perspective. They recognize that the church does not need an ecclesiastical priest to represent itself before God* (as distinct from Roman Catholic teaching). Jesus Christ is the "great high priest" (Heb. 4:14; 9:11) from whom the church's priesthood derives. All Christians are priests—coming before God and representing God to others. Thus, the priesthood of all believers is an image of the whole church of Jesus Christ.

An implication of recognizing all Christians as priests is that "ministers" in the church are not just ordained clergy but all church members, who are "priests." All Christians can carry out ministries to and in the world and for other persons. This is their responsibility as priests. For instance, there are ministries of listening to others, hearing their needs and even confessions of sin*. Christian priests listen to others because God listens to us.

Ministries of helping emerge at every point in life. In countless ways, Christian priests can help others—in things both "great" and "small." This requires "priests" willing to have their own schedules interrupted to help others when needs arise. Helping others is love in action.

Ministries of bearing enable Christian priests to follow Paul's command: "Bear one another's burdens, and in this way you will fulfill the law*of Christ" (Gal. 6:2). Ministries of bearing know no limits, no boundaries. All persons are those whose burdens can be shared. The whole work of Christ can be summed up by "bear": "Surely he has borne our griefs and carried our sorrows . . ." (Isa. 53:4–5).

Princeton Theology

From the eighteenth to the early twentieth century, the theologians at Princeton Theological Seminary taught a developed form of Reformed Orthodoxy* that conveyed a scholastic form of the Reformed Protestant tradition*. The influence of the "old Princeton" theology was substantial throughout Reformed communities in the United States.

The earliest theologians in this tradition were Archibald Alexander, Samuel Miller, and Charles Hodge. They were followed by Joseph Addison Alexander, James Waddell Alexander, and others. A third generation was comprised of Archibald Alexander Hodge, Benjamin B. Warfield, Francis L. Patton, and J. Gresham Machen.

The founding professor, Archibald Alexander, combined a stalwart Reformed theology* with an emphasis on personal piety*. He learned Scottish Common Sense Realism as a student and it became an enduring "old Princeton" philosophy.

Princeton theologians sought to convey the Reformed theological heritage in its Presbyterian expression to Protestant America, through and beyond the period of the Civil War. This heritage embraced the teachings of John Calvin*, the Westminster Confession* (1647), and the theological formulations of the Reformed Orthodox, particularly Francis Turretin, whose three-volume textbook was used as the theology text for many years at the seminary. When Charles Hodge's *Systematic Theology* (3 vols., 1871–1873) was published, it became the hallmark and symbol of the "old Princeton" theology.

Hodge's son, A. A. Hodge, "popularized" his father's work in *Outlines of Theology* (1866, 1878), while his joint article with Warfield on biblical inspiration and inerrancy (published in *Presbyterian Review*, 1881) provided an ongoing defense of this feature of Reformed Orthodoxy. Warfield's own writings were extensive. They emphasized the Reformed theological tradition as well as apologetic efforts that have been influential beyond Presbyterian and Reformed bodies.

The Princeton theology was dissipating by the beginning of the twentieth century in the midst of a secularizing society, denominational conflicts over biblical authority*, and evolving philosophical viewpoints. The 1929 reorganization of the seminary led to a more diverse faculty.

Providence of God

God* maintains, guides, and is continually involved with the creation* and humanity* in order to carry out God's divine will and purposes in history*.

Christian believers are aware of God's providential activities in many realms of life. Without God's sustaining providence in upholding creation, all would fall into chaos. God's divine power continues to uphold, just as it created all things "in the beginning" (Gen. 1:1).

God's providence in carrying out God's plan and purposes involve the cooperation of humans. As humans live, make decisions, and take actions, God's ongoing providence cooperates with humans. Reformed theology* emphasizes God as the "first cause" of all things, and through God, humans are active as "secondary causes" as they cooperate with God. God works out the divine purposes through the actions and activities of humans, whether or not they are aware of God's providence. So human actions matter! Christian believers may not know or understand God's providential actions; they are a "mystery." But Christians live in faith*, believing "all things work together for good for those who love God, who are called according to his purpose" (Rom. 8:28). This promise is the believer's great comfort and solace, in all times, even when things are not clear. As John Preston wrote, a person "cannot see round about all the corners of Gods Providence" (Breastplate 282).

God's providence embraces God's government of nature, the world, and all persons. God has purposes for human history and beyond. All emerges from God's will, and God works through all things to accomplish God's ultimate ends (Eph. 1:9–12; Phil. 2:9–11). Biblically, images of the final "Kingdom of God*" or "reign of God" affirm that God's purposes will prevail. This is the vision: God "will reign forever and ever" (Rev. 11:15).

R

Racism

Discrimination on the basis of race is a problem worldwide. Racial groups within a society face injustice and ill treatment and are victims of wide-ranging forms of discrimination as well as violence against them.

The Presbyterian Church in Canada declared, "Racism is a sin*, incompatible with Jesus' teachings and a blatant denial of the Christian faith*." This statement is an important summary of Reformed theological understandings about the nature of racism and why it must be condemned. Theologically, the Confession of 1967 says, "God* has created the peoples of the earth to be one universal family" and in God's "reconciling love," God "overcomes the barriers" between people and "breaks down every form of discrimination based on racial or ethnic difference, real or imaginary" (BC 9.44). The Confession of Belhar* (1982) indicates that since "God has entrusted the church* with the message of reconciliation in and through Jesus Christ*" (10.5), the confession rejects "any doctrine* which . . . sanctions in the name of the gospel or of the will of God the forced separation of people on the grounds of race and color," since this "obstructs and weakens the ministry* and experience of reconciliation in Christ" (10.6).

These statements provide theological groundings for understanding the sinfulness of racism. A counter to racism, in the context of the condition of apartheid in South Africa, was the Confession of Belhar's emphases on themes of unity, reconciliation, and justice*. The implication, as "A Brief Statement of Faith" says, of God's creating the world "good" and making "everyone equally in God's image, male and female, of every race and people, to live as one community" (BC 11.3) means racism in any form cannot be tolerated and must be condemned as sinful in the sight of God. Reformed churches adhering to these confessional statements are charged with living out their churches' antiracist convictions.

Regeneration

Reformed theology* understands regeneration as the "rebirth of mind and will accomplished by the gracious work of the Holy Spirit* at the outset of the *ordo salutis*" (*DGLTT* 259).

"Rebirth" describes the "new creation" (2 Cor. 5:17) of those God* has elected for salvation*. The "new person" in Jesus Christ* receives the gift of faith* in justification* in which sin* is forgiven. The righteousness of Jesus Christ is received so that one has a new standing before God, being united with Christ by faith. Regeneration precedes faith, repentance*, and conversion*, and leads to sanctification*. These are responses to God's gracious mercy in Christ.

John Calvin* emphasized that salvation is "a free gift [cf. Eph. 2:5], because the beginning of every good is from the second creation, which we attain in Christ" (*Inst.* 2.3.6). Regeneration is "the beginning of the spiritual life" (cf. John 1:13; 1 Pet. 1:23).

Regeneration is linked to God's election* and predestination* to salvation of the elect, since regeneration occurs only in the elect. Regeneration is related to sin since in regeneration God brings new life to a sinner, with the sinful will being changed from "an evil to a good will" (*Inst.* 4.3.6). As Calvin said, "Everything good in the will is the work of grace* alone." Regeneration is joined to sanctification. The regenerate grow in faith and holiness by God's Spirit as they serve God as disciples of Jesus Christ.

Reformed theology stresses regeneration as the work of God's grace, alone. This contrasts with Arminianism, where the unaided human will is seen as able to turn to God, a kind of moral readjustment. The "Enthusiasts" believed "enthusiastical raptures" and "ecstasies" were a regenerating work of the Spirit. But for the Reformed, God is the "author of the spiritual life from beginning to end" (*Inst.* 2.3.6).

Repentance

The Heidelberg Catechism (1563) asks: "What is involved in genuine repentance or conversion*?" and answers: "Two things: the dying-away of the old self, and the rising-to-life of the new" (BC 4.088; Rom. 6:4–6; Eph. 4:22–24). This double action is the work of the Holy Spirit* as those who are regenerate* become a "new creation" (2 Cor. 5:17). The Catechism continues: "Q. What is the dying-away of the old self? A. To be genuinely sorry for sin* and more and more to hate and run away from it. Q. What is the rising-to-life of the new self? A. Wholehearted joy in God* through Christ and a love and delight to live according to the will of God by doing every kind of good work" (BC 4.089–90; Q. 88–90).

Repentance is a process through the work of the Holy Spirit. Heinrich Bullinger* in the Second Helvetic Confession (1566) wrote that "repentance is a gift of God" and "not a work of our own strength" (BC 5.094). The Spirit enables believers to "lament sins committed" (5.094). It is not "penance" God requires—as in Roman Catholic theology—but "repentance" as true sorrow. This leads to one who confesses sins to God. Sin is hated and "run away" from, joined with "a firm purpose to follow good" (Marrow 160). Repentance is the response to God's loving mercy and thus follows from faith* (Inst. 3.3.19–21).

Karl Barth* saw conversion and repentance as a "quarrel, or falling-out," with one's old self. One "renounces what he previous was and did, leaving his old way." Now one enters "a completely new and different being and action, entering a new way," which "opens up" in freedom* (CD IV/2, 570). One's existence and being is now driven by "the powerful truth that God is for him and he is for God" in Jesus Christ* (571).

Resurrection

"We arise because Christ arose," wrote John Calvin* (1 Cor. 15:12ff.; *Inst.* 3.25.7). The resurrection of Jesus Christ* is a central tenet of Christianity, affirmed as in faith* by the Nicene and Apostles' Creeds* and considered by the Reformed to be the first step in Christ's exaltation after his death*.

The cause of Christ's resurrection is the power of God*. Christ's human nature takes on new life in order to bring salvation* to believers. William Ames indicated the purposes of Christ's resurrection: (1) to show Christ as the Son of God (Rom. 1:4); (2) to seal Christ's victory over death (1 Cor. 15:57); (3) to fulfill the parts of Christ's office that followed his death; (4) to show himself justified and justifying others (1 Cor. 15:17); and (5) to be the substance, example, and beginning of our spiritual and bodily resurrection (1 Cor. 15:20, 21, 23). These dimensions of Christ's resurrection show "Christ as God is absolutely and in principle the cause of our resurrection" (*Marrow* 146). Christ's resurrection was "the prelude to the resurrection for which we hope*, or rather a pledge of it" (*Inst.* 3.25.7).

In the future resurrection for humanity*, "our corruptible nature will be destroyed," wrote Calvin, and "there will be a sudden transition from our corruptible nature to blessed immortality" (Comm. 1 Cor. 15:51; CNTC 9:343). Believers now have this resurrection hope, which sustains throughout their lives of service to God, "so that they do not fall out of the race" (1 Cor. 15:58). They are "resting on an unshakeable foundation, when they know that a better life is ready, waiting for them, in heaven*" (CNTC 9:348). Calvin wrote, movingly, "Christ rose again that he might have us as companions in the life to come" (*Inst.* 3.25.3).

Revelation

God's* self-disclosure to humanity* is a revealing of the truth about God, which has been concealed or unknown. God must be the source and content of revelation, since God's divine will must be the originator of conveying all knowledge of God*.

Reformed theology* has recognized general revelation (also called natural theology*), referring to a revelation of God in nature, the created order, or moral consciousness. Yet while some have argued there can be some "knowledge of God" conveyed in general revelation, Reformed theology acknowledges this knowledge is not a knowledge of God's character, who God is and what God has done, especially in relation to humanity.

For John Calvin*, while believing in a "sense of divinity*" in all people (*Inst.* 1.3.1), this "seed of religion" (1.4.1) is smothered by sin* so "all degenerate from the true knowledge" of God. Thus "no real piety* exists in the world."

God's special revelation is in the Scriptures*. The Bible is God's revelation of who God is and what God has done, especially in providing salvation* to sinful humanity in Jesus Christ*. In him, God's Word and God's will are revealed (John 1:1, 14). Karl Barth* said, "God is who he is in his works; . . . in his works he is himself revealed as the one he is" (*CD* II/1, 260). The "hidden God" is made "apprehensible" (199) in Jesus Christ who is "the self-revealing God" (I/1, 384).

Jesus Christ is God incarnate*, "God with us" (Matt. 1:23). God's revelation in Christ is known through the Scriptures, the Word of God*, by the work of the Holy Spirit*. The Spirit brings faith* in Christ and also faith that Scripture is God's Word. Preaching* the "good news" of Jesus Christ is a form of the Word of God, as God's acts and will are made known (*BC* 5.004).

S

Sacraments

Reformed theology* recognizes two sacraments: baptism* and the Lord's Supper*. Both are sacraments since they are instituted by God* as visible and outward "signs" and "seals" of divine grace*. Sacraments are means of grace and outward expressions of God's covenant* promises, focused in Jesus Christ*. Sacraments are "a visible word" of God (Augustine). The Word of God* gives sacraments their meaning. Sacraments appeal to sight, touch, and taste to show and convey God's gracious promises to God's people through faith*. For John Calvin*, they are "mirrors in which we may contemplate the riches of God's grace, which he lavishes upon us" (*Inst.* 4.14.6).

Baptism is linked to the Old Testament* practice of circumcision (Gen. 17:11; Col. 2:11–12) as expressing entry into the "household of God" as part of God's covenant people. Baptism is administered in the name of the Trinity* and marks the baptized as a member of Christ's body in the church*—in both infant and adult baptism.

The Lord's Supper is linked to Old Testament Passover celebrations (Exod. 12:7–8, 13; 23:14–17; 1 Cor. 5:7). The Supper celebrates Jesus Christ as the "new covenant" (1 Cor. 11:25) who died for our sins* (Rom. 5:8). Christ brings new life and salvation* by the power of the Holy Spirit*.

Reformed theology adopted Augustine's view of a sacrament as "a sign and the thing signified." These exist together in a "spiritual relation, or sacramental union" between "the sign and the thing signified" (BC 6.151). Calvin, distinct from Huldrych Zwingli*, maintained that sacraments are more than "memorials." They are signs and seals where God's grace is "represented, presented, and applied" by the Holy Spirit, said William Ames (*Marrow* 197). Sacraments "seal the whole covenant of grace to believers . . . not only at the time they are administered but to the end of life" (198).

Salvation

God's* actions to rescue and liberate humanity* from its bondage to sin* (Rom. 5:12–14) through the life, death*, and resurrection* of Jesus Christ*. "Salvation" (Gr. *soteria*) restores the relationship of love and trust intended for humans to God but ruptured by sin to make humanity*, by nature, alienated, guilty, and "enemies" (Rom. 5:10) of God. Theologically, this is called Soteriology.

Through Christ's death, the power of sin is overcome by God's love. Sin is forgiven, and eternal life with God in heaven* is given to those who have faith*. John Calvin* wrote, "We have in his death the complete fulfillment of salvation, for through it we are reconciled to God, his righteous judgment* is satisfied, the curse is removed, and the penalty paid in full" (*Inst.* 2.16.13). "In rising again," Christ "came forth victor over death, so the victory of our faith over death lies in his resurrection alone" (2.16.13).

Salvation is by God's grace*—for "God so loved the world that he gave his only Son . . ." (John 3:16). Salvation is received through faith, which Calvin defined as "a firm and certain knowledge of God's benevolence toward us, founded upon the truth of the freely given promise in Christ, both revealed to our minds and sealed upon our hearts through the Holy Spirit*" (*Inst.* 3.2.6). Salvation is the work of the Holy Spirit, who gives faith by which "the promise of salvation penetrates into our minds" (3.1.4), for "faith itself has no other source than the Spirit" (3.1.4).

Through faith, forgiveness* of sin is found (Col. 1:14). Freedom* from the condemning power of the law* (Rom. 3:20) is given; and reconciliation between God and humanity is achieved (2 Cor. 5:16–21). Salvation brings receiving "God's generosity" in justification* but also the grace of sanctification*, by which the Spirit leads believers to continuing repentance* and holiness and obedience to God.

Sanctification

Sanctification is the theological condition and process of a Christian's being made holy and growing in the life of faith* and obedience to God* in Jesus Christ*.

Protestant theology teaches that sanctification follows justification*. God declares a sinner righteous through the death* and resurrection* of Jesus Christ, which brings salvation* by God's grace* through faith. Sanctification is growth in faith as Christians live in obedience to God's Word and God's will for their lives.

Justification is an event, while sanctification is a process, never completed in this life. In justification, a sinner's status is changed before God. In sanctification, the sinner, who is now declared righteous in God's sight, experiences a change in the nature of the person. In sanctification, the Christian's whole self is changed, now to focus on cleansing from sin* and growing in Christ (Eph. 4:15), by loving and serving God and others.

Reformed theology* emphasizes sanctification is the work of God's Holy Spirit*. The Spirit leads and guides believers into God's ways— known through the reading of Scripture*, the preaching* of the Word of God*, and prayer*. Reformed theology stresses that believers obey God's Law*, since the law expresses God's will. The Spirit works in believers who cooperate with the Spirit. Believers' efforts to do good works as expressions of faith are the work of God's Spirit. These works of love, care, and justice* serve others and give practical expression to one's confession of Jesus Christ as Lord and Savior. God's grace in salvation frees believers to live "in the Spirit" who dwells in them (Rom. 8:9).

Sanctification is not a "second blessing" or "special experience." Sanctification takes shape day by day as believers seek lives of faithful obedience to the God who loves them and saves them by grace through faith in Jesus Christ. Daily, one does all for the glory of God (1 Cor. 10:31)!

Schleiermacher, Friedrich Daniel Ernst

Friedrich Daniel Ernst Schleiermacher (1768–1834) was a German minister, preacher, and theologian. He was ordained in the Reformed Church in 1794. In his *On Religion: Speeches to Its Cultured Despisers* (1799; Eng. 1894), Schleiermacher argued for the place of religious experience as the defining essence of religion. In 1809, he became pastor of Trinity Church and professor of theology at the new University of Berlin. He helped organize the Evangelical Church of the Prussian Union, which was a union of Lutheran and Reformed churches.

Schleiermacher's classic theological work was *The Christian Faith* (1821–1822; 2nd ed. 1830–1831; Eng. 1928). He hoped to reformulate theology in a post-Enlightenment world and saw doctrines* as historical formulations to be constantly criticized and revised. Schleiermacher critiqued traditional theological language to reconstruct theology.

Theology is a re-thematizing of the experience of redemption in Jesus Christ*. It can be said that "the Gospel, for Schleiermacher, is that the divine being unites with human nature in the person of Christ, such that the creation* of human nature comes to completion in Christ, and thereby establishes the reign of God* on earth" (*OHRT* 321). The divine essence is expressed through a person's consciousness of Christ, who is the "new Adam," the completion of human nature. Christ is distinguished from all others by "the steady strength of his God-consciousness, a strength that was an actual being of God in him" (*CF* 574).

Human nature finds its completion in Christ's redeeming work. In this, humanity* is brought into the "community of his activity and life" (*CF* 622). Said Schleiermacher, "The Redeemer takes up persons of faith* into the strength of his God-consciousness, and this is his redeeming activity" (621). "Being united with Christ," wrote Schleiermacher, "is the actual possession of blessedness in consciousness that Christ is the focus of our life" (631).

Scripture

Holy Scripture as the Word of God* written has been a primary theological conviction of Reformed theology*. Various formulations of the meaning of this statement have been given. The canon* of Scripture is agreed: the thirty-nine books of the Old Testament* and the twenty-seven books of the New Testament*. Scripture is the means by which we come to a knowledge of God* and through which God's plan for salvation* in Jesus Christ* is revealed. Scripture is God's authoritative Word because it is God's special revelation*, our only place to learn of God's actions and will. Scripture has primacy over all other sources of knowledge: tradition*, reason*, and religious experience.

Reformed confessions* describe Scripture as "the Word of God" written (BC 5.003, 6.002). The Reformed recognize that "the Bible is both a human witness to revelation and revelation itself through human words" (Holy Scripture 70). Karl Barth* understood the function of Scripture to be to "witness" to God's Word in Jesus Christ. Scripture's authority* is grounded in "the witness of the Holy Spirit*" (CD I/2, 537)" which gives Scripture its special content since "there is no other book which witnesses to Jesus Christ apart from Holy Scripture" (IV/1, 368). Jesus Christ is encountered in Scripture by the work of the Holy Spirit.

Scripture is "inspired by God" (2 Tim. 3:16–17). God is the "author" of Scripture, using humans "moved by the Holy Spirit" (2 Pet. 1:20–21) to convey the message God desired. Scripture's purpose (scopus) and the purpose of its inspiration to be the "rule of faith* and life" (BC 6.002).

Some Reformed have spoken of Scripture as "inerrant," as being completely accurate in all it teaches—including science and history*. Others have used "infallible" to indicate that Scripture will not lie or deceive about Scripture's focus: God's salvation in Jesus Christ.

Sense of Divinity

John Calvin* used the term *sensus divinitatis* (Lat. "sense of divinity") to refer to an awareness of God* that is naturally implanted in humans (*Inst.* 1.3.1; also "seed of religion," "sense of deity").

Calvin saw this as "beyond controversy," and it is a guard against "anyone . . . taking refuge in the pretense of ignorance." Implanted in all is "a certain understanding of his divine majesty" and "all perceive that there is a God and that he is their Maker."

The upshot of this is that "a sense of divinity which can never be effaced is engraved upon men's minds" (*Inst.* 1.3.3), yet "all degenerate from the true knowledge of [God]," so "no real piety* remains in the world" (1.4.1). While they "ought" to "break forth into praises of him," they are "actually puffed up and swollen with all the more pride." Knowledge of God* is smothered or corrupted and hypocrisy reigns. Humans "have not been utterly ignorant of God," but "what should have come forth sooner was held back by stubbornness" (1.4.4).

Each person's mind, wrote Calvin, "is like a labyrinth" and "scarcely a single person has ever been found who did not fashion for himself an idol or specter in place of God" (*Inst.* 1.5.12). Smothering this knowledge of God renders humans "inexcusable" (1.5.14), for "all excuse is cut off because the fault of dullness is within us" (1.5.15). Humans "corrupt the seed of the knowledge of God, sown in their minds out of the wonderful workmanship of nature" and this "must be imputed to their own failing." This is human sin*.

Calvin said it is the "spectacles" of Scripture* that "clearly shows us the true God" (1.6.1). When the knowledge of God the Creator fails to bring salvation*, the knowledge of God the Redeemer—Jesus Christ*—is needed.

Sin

Sin is a basic biblical concept referring to the condition of human nature being alienated from its Creator, God*. Sin, according to Martin Luther, is humans beings "turned in upon themselves" (LW 345) so they follow their own will and desires instead of obeying God's will. Humans' relationship with God is not one of trust and love. Humans are corrupted and estranged from God. Sin affects human relationships with each other and with nature. The Westminster Shorter Catechism (1648) succinctly says, "Sin is any want of conformity unto, or transgression of, the law* of God" (BC 7.014).

The "image of God*" in which humanity* was created (Gen. 1:27) was defaced and corrupted by the "fall into sin" (Gen. 3). The seriousness of sin is a consistent biblical warning. Sin's consequences include guilt before God, the condition of wickedness, and the facing of ultimate punishment (Ps. 91:8) and spiritual death* (Rom. 5:12).

Sin is "original sin*," which refers to humanity's* sinfulness in its "origins" (Ps. 51:5). Original sin is a "habitual deviation of the whole nature of man, or a turning aside from the law of God," wrote William Ames (Marrow 120). This corruption is pervasive, affecting the whole of a person—mind, will, and heart. All humans are born with a sinful nature, which is incapable of turning toward God by its own power or own will. Only an act of God can obliterate original sin.

Actual sins are the sins committed by sinful humans, particularly violations of the law of God (as represented in the Ten Commandments). Sins of commission are sinful actions. Sins of omission are failures to act when one should act in obedience to God's will.

Christ's death on the cross is the atonement* through which sin can be forgiven, salvation* received, and a person become a "new creation."

Social Gospel

The Social Gospel was a movement in the United States (1870–1913) focused on the social problems of the nation related to developments of important forces such as industrialization, urbanization, and immigration. Ministers became involved in seeking to redress conditions relating to health, labor, housing, and urban renewal. Various media called attention to the plight of workers and cities. Capitalism was seen as creating extreme struggles with the social conditions of Americans, particularly the poor.

Baptists (Walter Rauschenbusch and William Newton Clarke) and Congregationalists (Washington Gladden and Josiah Strong) were leaders of this movement. These denominations can be understood as parts of the Reformed family. The largest Presbyterian denomination, the Presbyterian Church in the United States of America, struggled with tensions between "old Calvinist" theology and a "new theology" more focused on contemporary social life. This dynamic, combined with the power of urban Presbyterians, who in this period were usually of the upper social and economic classes, helped maintain a conservative Presbyterian stance resistant to wide changes in the status quo.

In 1910, however, the church's* General Assembly* issued a fourteen-point Declaration on Social Principles. This sought to apply the principles of the Kingdom of God* to modern life and urged that "the Church is under imperative obligation to show how these Christian principles apply to human affairs" (*Minutes* 230). Among its points, the Declaration called for the abolition of child labor, abatement of poverty, safer working conditions, a shorter workweek, arbitration in industrial disputes, an acknowledgment of the responsibilities of wealth, and a more equitable distribution of wealth. Ministers were to recognize their obligations "with respect to the social application" of the Gospel, and church members were to study social problems seriously and participate in "social service" (*Minutes* 230–32). These were also emphases of the Social Gospel agenda.

Stewardship

"Steward" is a biblical term (Gr. *oikonomos*) used to describe one who is entrusted with the properties of another person. It points to the accountability to manage or use another's property responsibly.

The theological concept of "stewardship" relates to the responsibilities humans are given for creation* by God* (Gen. 1:28; 2:15). It also points toward the responsibilities given to the church* of Jesus Christ* to carry out God's mission in the world (1 Cor. 4:1–2). Those who are "good stewards of the manifold grace* of God" are to "serve one another with whatever gift each of you has received" (1 Pet. 1:10).

Some have indicated that stewardship can be a primary biblical metaphor for Christian faith* and life itself: "Stewardship is my life!" Stewardship is a vocation* to which all Christians are called as they "serve one another." More broadly, our stewardship is in how humans (and nations) relate to the earth itself and meet issues such as climate change, pollution, and caring for others in the face of natural disasters. The human family—and especially Christians—are accountable for the ways we use natural resources and for "creation care*" as responsible stewards of God's gift of the earth.

Confessional expressions of the importance of stewardship are found in "A Brief Statement of Faith," which says, "We violate the image of God* in others and ourselves, accept lies as truth, exploit neighbor and nature, and threaten death* to the planet entrusted to our care. We deserve God's condemnation" (BC 35–39). The implications of poor stewardship of creation are highlighted by the Christian Reformed Church: "Beyond the direct effects on 'the environment*,' our failure as stewards of creation also impacts the wellbeing of other humans, particularly the poor, the hungry, and the powerless, who God has called us to aid" (*Creation*).

Supralapsarianism

Supralapsarianism was a viewpoint from a post-Reformation controversy within Reformed theology* relating to the ordering of the divine decrees*.

Supralapsarianism stood counter to infralapsarianism* on the place of the fall into sin* in the purposes of God*, known as the divine decrees. Supralapsarianism (Lat. *supra lapsum*) meant "above" or "prior to the fall." It is sometimes said to be a full "double predestination*" compared to the infralapsarian position, which has been called "single predestination."

In the supralapsarian view, God's eternal decrees of election* and reprobation* from all eternity were "above" (Lat. *supra*) or "preceded" the creation* of humans. The decree was issued by God whether or not humans were sinners, since it was issued before their creation. Thus, decrees of election and reprobation of individuals are (logically) prior to the divine decree of creation and God's decision to permit humanity's* fall into sin. The object of predestination in supralapsarianism is humanity not yet created and not yet fallen into sin. The logical and temporal order of God's divine decrees is the reverse of the infralapsarian view, which taught a temporal order of creation, fall, and salvation*.

Supralapsarianism sought to protect God's "sovereignty," since God's highest purpose was to glorify God in the salvation of persons who are "elect." The critique is that supralapsarianism made the Fall a necessary means to God's decreeing salvation. This could also be construed as making God the author of sin.

Theodore Beza first formulated supralapsarianism. It was also promoted by Franciscus Gomarus. Most Reformed theologians have been infralapsarian. Karl Barth* argued that supralapsarianism should not be understood as an absolute "decree," which made election and reprobation equal, "symmetrical" decrees. For Barth, Jesus Christ* was the true object of predestination. Christ himself was the divine decree and is "the election of God before which and without which and beside which God cannot make any other choices" (*CD* II/2, 94).

T

Theology, Reformed

Reformed theology designates a stream of Reformation theology associated with theologians who differed from Martin Luther and emerging Lutheranism as well as from the Anabaptist movements of the time.

Reformed theologians include John Calvin*, Huldrych Zwingli*, Heinrich Bullinger*, and Martin Bucer* in the sixteenth century. As theological perspectives developed in the seventeenth century, Reformed Orthodoxy* marked the summation, systematization, and elaboration of these earlier theologies. Reformed Orthodox theologians include Theodore Beza, Zacharias Ursinus, Caspar Olevianus, Girolamo Zanchi, and Francis Turretin.

In the nineteenth century, Friedrich Daniel Ernst Schleiermacher* sought to relate Reformed doctrines* to new intellectual and cultural contexts. In the United States, the theologians at Princeton Seminary, including Charles Hodge and B. B. Warfield, maintained Reformed theology with Reformed Orthodox emphases. In Europe, strong Reformed theology was upheld by Dutch theologians Abraham Kuyper and Herman Bavinck. In the twentieth century, Karl Barth* believed Reformed theology must be continually reformed by God's Word* and developed his extensive theology accordingly.

Reformed theology seeks to be biblical, expounded under the authority* of Scripture*. One might characterize a basic impulse of Reformed theology as stressing the initiative of God* in all things. Throughout its development of theological doctrine*, Reformed theology emphasizes God "making the first move." God reveals, God sends Jesus Christ*, God elects persons for salvation*, God establishes the church*, God leads and guides. All these and other Christian doctrines seek to give glory to God in praise and thanks for what God has done. Specific theological formulations of Reformed theology express the work of God in relation to humanity* as the sovereign Lord, who loves in Jesus Christ and gives grace* through the Holy Spirit*. Historic controversies—as with Arminianism—display this emphasis on God's initiative at every point.

William Ames wrote, "Theology is the doctrine or teaching [*doctrina*] of living to God" (*Marrow* 77). Reformed theology, in its totality, concerns "faith*" and "observance"—what to believe and how to live.

Tradition

Tradition (Lat. *traditio*, from *tradere*: "to hand over") relates to what has been "handed over" from the past to the present and what the present time receives from the past. This can take numerous forms. Reformed theology*, like other theological traditions, chooses what to receive as "tradition" in positive ways and what parts of "tradition" to neglect or reject.

A sixteenth-century Reformation-era contention was over the question of authority*: Where does the church* or theology receive authority? Roman Catholics believed the Scriptures* and it's church's tradition were co-sources of authority. Protestants (and Reformed) believed Scripture alone is the source of authority for the church. This meant that Protestants rejected Roman Catholic ecclesiastical traditions they did not believe were grounded in Scripture. The Second Helvetic Confession (1566) said, "We reject human traditions, even if they be adorned with high-sounding titles, as though they were divine and apostolical" (*BC* 5.014).

Doctrinal authority for the Reformed was found in the teachings of the early and medieval churches—when they accorded with proper theological understandings based on the Scriptures. John Calvin*, along with other Reformed theologians, drew positively from some teachings of Augustine; other parts of Augustine they rejected. Other predecessor theologians from the church's tradition were appropriated in varying degrees depending on the issue.

When it came to biblical interpretation, Calvin often wrote disparagingly about "traditions," but he was "consciously in conversation with a living historical discourse on the meaning of the scriptural text" (*CCT* 45–46; cf. 43). Calvin looked to the early church theologian John Chrysostom as a kind of "exegetical tutor" on a number of important biblical and interpretive matters (166–70).

Reformed theology has been committed to the authority of Scripture, but elements of "tradition" also find their places at some points.

Trinity

The one eternal God* is one Being in three persons: Father, Son, and Holy Spirit*. This understanding was hammered out in the centuries of the early church* in "trinitarian controversies" where various ways of articulating the reality of the God whom Christians worship* were explored. By the fourth century, the Western church spoke of the Godhead as three coequal persons who share the same "substance" or "essence" (Gr. *ousia*; Lat. *substantia*). These three persons are one God.

Reformed theology* appropriated the understandings of the Western church. In their doctrines* of God, a number of theologians went into great detail about the divine essence and attributes (see GMG). Since the Trinity is central to Christian theology, it was important for precise theological understandings to be considered.

In the twentieth century, Karl Barth* made the Trinity his key theological theme in developing his doctrines* of Revelation* and theological anthropology. To avoid contemporary misunderstandings by modern interpreters, Barth spoke of one God in "three distinctive modes of being" (*CD* I §9, 348). The "threeness is grounded in the one essence of the revealed God" (I/1, 360). The doctrine of the Trinity is "the unity of God in the three modes of being of Father, Son and Holy Ghost, or of the threefold otherness of the one God in the three modes of being of Father, Son and Holy Ghost" (375). The one God is the revealer, the revelation, and the effect of this revelation.

Jürgen Moltmann* stressed the Trinity as a divine community, which became a model for human communities (political and ecclesiastical). Letty Russell indicated that the image of "partnership" (Gr. *koinonia*) as displaying mutuality, reciprocity, and a totally shared life is conveyed by the doctrine of the Trinity. Humans are set free to live in partnership with each other and with God in shared life.

U

Ubiquity

A controversy between the Lutherans and the Reformed about the universal presence of Jesus Christ*: Does the universal presence of Jesus Christ, in his divine nature, imply that Christ is also bodily present everywhere?

The Lutherans contended that Christ, in his glorified humanity, by the power of the Holy Spirit*, is present everywhere, bodily. This was crucial for Lutheran views of the Lord's Supper*, which stressed Christ's sacramental presence in relation to the physical elements of the Supper.

The Reformed view was that of John Calvin* (*Inst.* 4.17.16–31), who believed there is a "real" presence of Christ when the Supper is celebrated. But Calvin rejected the claim that Christ's body had the divine property of "ubiquity" (Lat. *ubique*: "everywhere"). For him, the Lutheran view threatened Christ's true humanity, within which— along with Christ's true divinity—salvation* rests. Calvin wrote that "placing the body itself in the bread, they assign to it a ubiquity con- trary to its nature, and by adding 'under the bread' mean that it lies hidden there . . . they insist on the local presence of Christ" (4.17.6).

Calvin believed it is wrong to think Christ is not "present" in the Supper "unless he comes down to us" (*Inst.* 4.17.31). Calvin said, "We do not think it lawful for us to drag him from heaven*." Calvin called ubiquity a "monstrous notion" (4.17.30). On Christ's human body, Calvin wrote that "by his ascension* into heaven he made it plain that it is not in all places, but when it passes into one, it leaves the previous one" (4.17.30; cf. 26). In the Supper, it is the "secret power of the Spirit" that is "the bond of our union with Christ*" (4.17.33). The "Spirit alone causes us to possess Christ completely and have him dwelling in us" (4.17.12). By the Spirit, Christ "lifts us up to himself" (4.17.16; cf. 18).

Union with Christ

Also called "Mystical Union" or "Spiritual Union," this is a special union grounded in God's* indwelling grace* in Jesus Christ* found between Christ and those who are regenerated* as Christian believers. Faith* established by the Holy Spirit* is the bond that unites.

Biblical images such as "I am the vine; you are the branches" (John 15:5), which speak of abiding in Christ, and the image of the church* as united in "one body" with its head, Jesus Christ (Eph. 4), show the elect being joined in a deep bond with Christ through faith. This union is established by God's grace and mercy, as is God's election* of the church and believers. This is a spiritual union, initiated and maintained by the Holy Spirit. Thus, Reformed theology* can define union with Christ as "the spiritual conjunction (coniunctio spiritualis) of the Triune God with the believer in and following justification*. It is a substantial and graciously effective indwelling" (DLGTT 314).

This union brings the benefits of the work of Christ of salvation* to believers. The sign and seal of this union is baptism*, in which there is an "ingrafting into Christ" (BC 6.154). This "secret union with the devout" is made visible in the Lord's Supper*, for "just as bread and wine sustain physical life, so are souls fed by Christ" (Inst. 4.17.1). The "purpose of this mystical blessing" is that "the Supper confirms for us" that "the Lord's body was once for all so sacrificed for us that we may now feed upon it, and by feeding feeling in ourselves the working of that unique sacrifice." This brings an assurance of eternal life (4.17.2).

Karl Barth* spoke of the goal of Christian calling* as an "attachment to Jesus Christ" and "fellowship" with Christ (CD IV/3/2, 528, 535).

Universalism

This stream of Christian theology has taught the final salvation* of all people: All will be forgiven for their sins* and be restored to live in everlasting fellowship with God*.

Universalism has emphasized the love of God for all people. Early church* proponents included Origen and Gregory of Nyssa. Universalism was strongly opposed by Augustine. During the Reformation, Anabaptist Hans Denck taught the doctrine*, but it was rejected by Lutheran and Reformed theologians. Since then, universalism has continued to be taught by various theologians.

The traditional Reformed view is that the kingdom of heaven* is "opened" to those who "accept the gospel promise in true faith*." But the kingdom of heaven is "closed" to "unbelievers . . . as long as they do not repent, the wrath of God and eternal condemnation rest on them" (BC 4.084; cf. 6.180, 181).

Karl Barth's* view of Jesus Christ* as the representative for all humanity* who dealt with sin in his death* as being simultaneously "elect" and "reprobate" raised the question of whether every human being will be saved.

Some have said Barth came to "the brink of universalism." His theological understandings led him in this direction, but he would not be drawn to make the final step on the eternal consequences of his views. He made two points. First, we cannot impinge on the freedom* of God to do what God wills. God *does not have* to save all people—as if God were bound to do so. Said Barth, "We must not arrogate to ourselves that which can be given and received only as a free gift" (CD IV/3/1, 477). Second, on the basis of Christ's work, however, we have this hope* for universal reconciliation* and can "pray cautiously": "There is no good reason why we should not be open to this possibility" (478).

V

Vocation

The term "vocation" (calling) is used in several senses in Reformed theology*.

Vocation (Lat. *vocatio*) as the call of God* to be God's children is a primary use of the term. There is an "external calling" to all persons in the universal call of the Gospel and an "internal calling" that is the inward calling of the Holy Spirit* to bring the elect to faith*. The "result of God's calling is the reception of believers into the kingdom and their union with and their life in Christ" (*DLGTT* 329).

In the church*, one may be called to an office, such as pastor.

Vocation also relates, as John Calvin* wrote, to how believers are to live out their Christian lives (sanctification*), for "the Lord bids each one of us in all life's actions to look to his calling." God has "appointed duties" for all persons in their "particular way of life." God calls all Christians to find their calling as "a sort of sentry post" so one does not "heedlessly wander about throughout life." This calling legitimates work* and occupations through which Christian faith can be expressed. For "the Lord's calling is in everything the beginning and foundation of well-doing" (*Inst.* 3.10.6).

This Reformed perspective imbues work with meaning. Labors can be recognized as valued ways of serving God, and "whatever you do, do everything for the glory of God" (1 Cor. 10:31). This applies to paying jobs as well as to the particular forms of service one renders to others as forms of ministry*. Calvin wrote on this verse that "there is no part of our life or conduct, however insignificant, which should not be related to the glory of God" (CNTC 9:224). Calvin recognized that callings may vary at different times in life, but this main purpose of life should be the Christian's guide.

W

War and Peace

War has been a fact of human existence, and armed conflicts are part of the Scriptures*. War brings hostilities and casualties leading to deaths, usually on a mass scale.

In its early sixteenth and seventeenth centuries, Reformed theology* considered war as one of the divinely ordained duties of "magistrates"—those kings and princes who in that time were seen as the agents of God* in governing nations. "Just war" theory developed as a means to "justify" wars. But "de facto, the major Reformation groups implicitly affirmed the just war theory, convinced that wars often had to be fought to support the right and oppose the wrong" (ERF 389). In "On Magistrates," the Second Helvetic Confession (1566) indicated that "if it is necessary to preserve the safety of the people by war, let him wage war in the name of God; provided he has first sought peace* by all means possible, and cannot save his people in any other way except by war" (BC 5.256). In this, the magistrate "serves God." These perspectives are shared in the Westminster Confession* (1647; 6.128).

In the current context, those holding Reformed theology often emphasize peace and peacemaking. A 1960 statement (reissued in 1980) by members of the faculty of the University of Dubuque Theological Seminary (Presbyterian) said that "the threat and exercise of the means of mass extermination in waging war is blasphemy against God the Creator, Preserver and Redeemer and is sin* against the creature for whom Christ died and rose again" (Mystery 168). The prospect of destroying the world and the planet has led many to a position of "nuclear pacifism," and the belief that "no 'good' coming out of a nuclear war could justify the destruction involved" (ERF 390).

Hope* anticipates the biblical vision: "Nation shall not lift up sword against nation; neither shall they learn war any more" (Isa. 2:4).

Westminster Confession of Faith

The Westminster Confession of Faith (1647) was part of the work of the Westminster Assembly (1643–1648). The Assembly was called by the "Puritan" Long Parliament to assemble "Divines" (theologians) to reform the Church of England to be "more agreeable to the Word of God*" (cited in Peter Toon, "Westminster Assembly," in *ERF* 392).

The Confession of Faith was produced along with a Larger and Shorter Catechism, a Directory for Public Worship, and Form of Church Government. While the Confession has had substantial influence since its writing in Reformed churches throughout the world, it did not have an important role in the future of Protestantism in England as a result of political developments.

The Confession conveys a consensus on Reformed theology* as modified by English Puritans. It builds on the work of Protestant reformers, chiefly Huldrych Zwingli*, John Calvin*, and Heinrich Bullinger*.

Among its important emphases are the role of Holy Scripture* as the "Word of God written" (*BC* 6.002), which has authority* and "ought to be believed and obeyed" (6.004) as "the rule of faith* and life" (6.002). God's* sovereignty is described in "Of God's Eternal Decrees" where God "from all eternity did by the most wise and holy counsel of his own will, freely and unchangeably ordain whatsoever comes to pass" (6.014). God's decree* is God's purpose and is a purpose for salvation*, for "the elect unto glory" (6.019), and "the passing by of others" (6.020) in the "high mystery of predestination*" (6.021).

God's covenant* expresses God's saving activity and is the concrete outworking of God's saving purposes. Humans are sinners "incapable of life" by obeying God's will (6.039). But in God's "covenant of grace*"—found in Jesus Christ* and his death* (6.040)—salvation is accomplished through Christ the mediator between God and humanity* (6.043). The Holy Spirit* gives faith (6.078) and "a new heart" and "spirit" (6.075) whereby Christians live holy lives for God's glory.

Witness of the Holy Spirit

The witness of the Holy Spirit (Lat. *testimonium Spiritus Sancti*; also "internal testimony") is an important element of Reformed theology*. A basic Protestant conviction is that Word and Spirit are inextricably bound up together. The Spirit points (witnesses) to the Word of God*, and the Word helps believers understand and interpret the work of the Spirit.

Reformed theology teaches that "our faith* and its assurance do not proceed from flesh and blood, that is to say, from natural powers within us, but are the inspiration of the Holy Ghost" (BC 3.12). Faith in Scripture* as the Word of God and faith in Jesus Christ* as one's Lord and Savior comes by the work of the Holy Spirit*. There is no other source or origin for faith—not human merit or effort. This means salvation* is solely from God* by the work of the Holy Spirit. The Spirit is the "Spirit of adoption*," witnessing "with our spirits that we are the children of God" (Rom. 8:15, 16). This regeneration* brings believers into the church*, the fellowship of faith. In this, they receive the benefits of Christ's death* and resurrection*, received by faith given by the Spirit.

The Spirit in the New Testament* does not "call attention" to the Spirit. The Spirit's work is to point to Jesus Christ as known in Scripture. The gifts and "fruit" of the Spirit for the church and for Christians are to point them to Christ and enable their service to God in Christ.

The witness of the Spirit in salvation and the life of faith (in sanctification*) is the means through which God's providence* is carried out. The Spirit brings and nourishes faith as the Spirit helps us interpret Scripture.

Word of God

"Word of God" has different meanings in Reformed theology*.

God's* eternal Word is the Second Person of the Trinity*, the divine Logos, the Son of God (John 1).

God's incarnate* Word is Jesus Christ*, the eternal Son of God who became human and is the mediator of salvation* for God's elect.

The inspired Word of God is Scripture*. The Bible is God's Word written. Scripture is God's divine message expressed in the words of the biblical writers under the inspiration of God's Holy Spirit*.

The Word proclaimed in preaching* is the Word of God (BC 5.004).

The internal Word of the Spirit is the "inner Word" of the witness of the Holy Spirit* to Scripture as the Word of God.

These dimensions of "Word of God" are related to each other. Jesus Christ as the Word of God is known through the Scriptures. Thus: "The one sufficient revelation* of God is Jesus Christ, the Word of God incarnate, to whom the Holy Spirit bears unique and authoritative witness through the Holy Scriptures, which are received and obeyed as the word of God written" (BC 9.27).

The Word of God is God speaking—in the person of Jesus Christ and in the words of Scripture. When God speaks, people listen! Karl Barth* wrote, "The Bible does not tell us how we are supposed to talk with God, but rather what God says to us" (WGT 25).

The contemporary way of God speaking is through preaching. When proclamation is based on Scripture, by the work of the Holy Spirit, God's Word comes to those who hear. Hearing the Word of God is to lead to obeying the Word of God. John Calvin* notes that "hearing" means "faith*" which is "situated, not in the ears, but in the heart" (CNTC 4:129).

Work

Work is seen in Reformed theology* as an expression of Christians' sanctification* by which they serve God* through their calling* as God's elect and their callings to "be wholly governed by the authority* of Christ" and "look to His glory as its aim." As John Calvin* continued, "All our endeavours shall start out from the invocation of Christ and serve His glory" (CNTC 11:354, on Col. 3:17; cf. 1 Cor. 10:31). For "in the Scriptures* 'calling' is a lawful way of life, for it is connected with God, who actually calls us" (9:153; on 1 Cor. 7:20).

Calvin believed "anyone who benefits human society by his industry . . . is not to be regarded as having no occupation" (CNTC 8:418; on 2 Thess. 3:10). Work glorifies God. It benefits others in the world and seeks to meet many human needs. Work enhances the life of the church* and communities in society.

William Ames noted the "occupations of life in their nature look to the common good" (Marrow 322). He wrote that "it is not enough that one should simply work: He must work for what is good, Eph. 4:28. Quietly and diligently let him follow an occupation which agrees with the will of God and the profit of men, 1 Thess. 4:11, 12; 2 Thess. 3:12." In God's "particular providence*," God assigns work as part of one's "kind of life" which is by "the nod of God" (323). In work, people are to "be intent on their calling and devote themselves to lawful and honourable occupations, without which human life is lacking in direction" (CNTC 8:420).

Work's "work" is to be involved with carrying out God's purposes in the world through efforts that benefit others and the whole human community. Work is a means of God's blessings "which gives us cause for thanksgiving" (CNTC 11:354).

World Religions

There are greatly different historical contexts between the period of the early Reformed theologians in the sixteenth century and the world of today. This relates specially to attitudes about world religions, comparing what was earlier known of other faiths and today's knowledge of world religions.

The early Reformed, with other Protestants, looked upon adherents of non-Christian religions as eternally lost since they did not acknowledge God's* revelation* in Jesus Christ* or the work of Christ for the forgiveness* of sins* and reconciliation* of sinners with God. Impetus for worldwide proclamation of the Gospel and mission work was fueled by this theological recognition.

Today, some Reformed theologians have spoken of "the wider work of God" and emphasize early biblical covenants* (Gen. 3:15–16; 9:8–17) as being "revelatory and salvific in meaning and as constituting the framework of the entire biblical story" (ERF 409).

The Confession of 1967 addresses this issue:

> The Christian finds parallels between other religions and his own and must approach all religions with openness and respect. Repeatedly God has used the insight of non-Christians to challenge the church* to renewal. But the reconciling word of the gospel is God's judgment* upon all forms of religion, including the Christian. The gift of God in Christ is for all [people]. The church, therefore, is commissioned to carry the gospel to all [persons] whatever their religion may be and even when they profess none. (BC 9.42)

"Witness" is important in looking at the world of faiths. Christians testify to the God they know in Jesus Christ by the power of the Holy Spirit*. Interreligious dialogue* enables discussions and respectful listening to other viewpoints of other religions. Reformed theology* believes in God's sovereign freedom* to act and do whatever God wills. So "witnessing" to Christian faith* is the Christian's joy—and duty.

Worship

Reformed theology* stresses the worship of God* as a central, necessary action of Christians. Public worship is the corporate gathering of God's people participating in actions of adoration and praise, reverence, prayer* and supplication, and thanksgiving. Worship rehearses salvation* history* as known through Scripture*. It celebrates God's activities in creation* and redemption: "The true God alone is to be adored and worshipped" (BC 5.023).

Throughout public worship, liturgical rubrics and language are used. Among the elements of Reformed worship are music and singing, symbolic actions, and times of silence for prayer. The community hears the Word of God* through Scripture reading, preaching*/sermons, sacraments*, song (hymnody*), and liturgical forms. Responses to the Word of God through offerings and other actions enable the congregation to express their commitments to God in Jesus Christ*, as moved by the Holy Spirit*. Reformed worship is to be grounded in Scripture as the community of faith* worships God as God desires.

While these biblical and theological elements are constant features of Reformed worship, contexts of the congregation's worship services are important. Churches in Africa, Asia, and Latin America that were established as missionary churches from Western Reformed churches may blend traditional elements with other forms and materials that emerge from their own settings. There are also Reformed churches that have been influenced by the charismatic movement and give expression to forms that arise from this experience.

Reformed worship is trinitarian in recognizing the full work of the triune God. Prayers are appropriately made to each of the Persons of the Trinity* and to God as Trinity. Celebrations of baptism* and the Lord's Supper* proceed with special liturgical forms, with practices within the rites themselves being varied among Reformed churches. The service of public worship equips the saints for the service of God.

~

Z

Zwingli, Huldrych

Huldrych (Ulrich) Zwingli (1484–1531) was a major Swiss Protestant Reformer. He attended the University of Basel and was ordained as a Roman Catholic priest, serving several parishes. He became People's (Preaching*) Priest at the Great Minster in Zurich in 1519.

Zwingli began to preach through the Gospel of Matthew. He grew in his understandings and became leader of the Reform movement in Switzerland. He joined with other reformers, including Oecolampadius, and composed tracts and confessions* of faith*.

Zwingli and Martin Luther confronted each other at the Colloquy of Marburg (1529). They could come to no agreement about the nature of the Lord's Supper* and the presence of Christ in the Supper, leading Luther to speak harshly to Zwingli. Zwingli's theology was influenced by Augustine and Luther. He had a strong doctrine* of God's* sovereignty in election*, saying that election is "so absolutely free that no account is taken in it of our works or merits" (*On Providence* 199–200). Zwingli demanded austerity (with no music) in worship*. Zwingli believed the bread and wine in the Supper were commemorations of Christ received by faith*; Jesus's words "This is my body" meant "This signifies my body."

Zwingli advocated a clear distinction between the two natures of Christ. Christ was resurrected according to his divine nature and is at "the right hand of the Father." According to his human nature, he could not be in the eucharistic elements since his ascended body is in a particular place (heaven*) and cannot be physically present in more than one place at a time—and not in the elements of the Supper as a "real presence."

Zwingli wrote vigorously against Anabaptists and defended infant baptism*. He accepted baptism and the Lord's Supper as the church's* two sacraments*. Zwingli was killed in the second battle of Kappel.

Zwinglianism

Zwinglianism is the theological movement emerging from the theology of Huldrych Zwingli*, which became a stream of Reformed theology* as distinct from Calvinism*, which looked to John Calvin* as its primary theological figure.

Zwinglianism emphasized simplicity in worship*, organized around the Word of God*. Scripture* was a primary focus, instead of the visual images that were part of the Roman Catholic tradition* and ethos. This carried through in the rejection of music and church* organs along with stained glass, statues, and visual depictions in church sanctuaries.

Central to Zwinglianism was preaching*. "Christ is the only way to salvation*," said Zwingli, and "all Christians should do their utmost that everywhere only the Gospel of Christ be preached" (RC 36, 37). Sermons were drawn from the Scriptures, which have clarity and power, as the Spirit of God is "illuminating and inspiring the words in such a way that the light of the divine content is seen in his own light" (Clarity and Certainty 78).

Zwinglianism was marked by Zwingli's views of the sacraments*. Baptism* is a mark of one's church membership and, in Zwingli's Zurich context, of civil society. The Lord's Supper* is a symbolic action stirring faith* in believers who are commemorating Christ's death* for salvation. Zwinglianism did not teach Christ's presence in the Supper in the ways of Calvin and Calvinism or Martin Luther and Lutheranism. His major emphasis was on the Supper as a joyous, celebratory "remembrance" of Christ's death.

Zwingli's successor as the chief pastor of the Zurich church, Heinrich Bullinger*, developed covenantal theology. Zwingli interpreted Scripture in light of God's graceful covenant*, a single history* of redemption centered in Jesus Christ*. The sacraments of baptism and the Lord's Supper were New Testament* expressions of circumcision and Passover in the Old Testament*. This led Zwinglianism to stress infant baptism as children became members of the covenant.

Annotated Bibliography

Allen, R. Michael. *Reformed Theology*. New York: T&T Clark, 2010.
Allen presents a clear discussion of the important theological doctrines as understood in Reformed theology.

Allen, Michael, and Scott R. Swain, eds. *The Oxford Handbook of Reformed Theology*. New York: Oxford University Press, 2020.
Here, prominent scholars provide thirty-seven essays on Reformed theology, in four parts—Contexts, Texts, Topics and Themes—and a conclusion.

Alston, Wallace M., Jr., and Michael Welker, eds. *Reformed Theology: Identity and Ecumenicity*. Grand Rapids, MI: William B. Eerdmans, 2003.
This is a collection of twenty-eight essays that seek to identify trends and motifs in Reformed thought and seek resources for church ecumenical enrichment.

Ames, William. *The Marrow of Theology*. Trans. John Dykstra Eusden. Boston: Pilgrim Press, 1968.
This is a classic, comprehensive presentation of Reformed theology by an influential seventeenth-century English Puritan theologian.

Balserak, Jon. *Calvinism: A Very Short Introduction*. New York: Oxford University Press, 2017.
This book provides a short but focused introduction to Calvin's life and thought, and the spread of his theology.

Barth, Karl. *The Theology of the Reformed Confessions*. Trans. and Annotated by Darrell L. Guder and Judith J. Guder. Columbia Series in Reformed Theology. Louisville, KY: Westminster John Knox Press, 2002.
Here are Barth's lectures on Reformed Confessions, indicating his perspectives on historic Reformed theology.
Beeke, Joel R., and Sinclair B. Ferguson, eds. *Reformed Confessions Harmonized*. Grand Rapids, MI: Baker, 1999.
This is a comparative presentation of Reformed Confessions on their theological doctrines.
Benedetto, Robert, and Donald K. McKim. *Historical Dictionary of Reformed Churches*. (1999; 2010; 3rd ed. forthcoming). Historical Dictionaries of Religions, Philosophies, and Movements. Lanham, MD: Rowman & Littlefield.
This reference work is an extensive treatment of Reformed churches, history, and Reformed theology, with succinct discussions of global Reformed theology and practices and detailed bibliographies.
Calvin, John. *Institutes of the Christian Religion*. Ed. John T. McNeill. Trans. Ford Lewis Battles. 2 vols. The Library of Christian Classics. Philadelphia: Westminster Press, 1960.
Calvin's work is a classic in Reformed theology. The *Institutes* have had far-reaching effects throughout history to the present time in presenting bases for Reformed theology.
Christian Reformed Church in North America. *Ecumenical Creeds and Reformed Confessions*. Grand Rapids, MI: CRC Publications, 1988.
This is a helpful collection of important creeds of the ecumenical church and selected Reformed Confessions.
Cochrane, Arthur C., ed., with New Introduction by Jack Rogers. *Reformed Confessions of the Sixteenth Century*. Louisville, KY: Westminster John Knox Press, 2003.
This is an important collection of sixteenth-century Reformed Confessions not available in other places. The New Introduction discusses the development of new confessions and continues to show the richness and clarity of the diverse Reformed theological tradition.
Dowey, Edward A., Jr. *A Commentary on the Confession of 1967 and an Introduction to the Book of Confessions*. Philadelphia: Westminster Press, 1968.
Dowey's book is a theological commentary on the Confession of 1967 and combined with theological analyses of other Confessions in *The Book of Confessions* of the Presbyterian Church in the United States of America.
Feldmeth, Nathan P., S. Donald Fortson III, Garth M. Rosell, and Kenneth J. Stewart. *Reformed and Evangelical across Four Centuries: The Presbyterian Story in America*. Grand Rapids, MI: William B. Eerdmans, 2022.

This is an up-to-date presentation of Presbyterianism in the United States from its earliest times until today. The authors represent four contemporary Presbyterian denominations and are evangelical in outlook.

Gerrish, B. A., ed. *Reformed Theology for the Third Christian Millennium.* Louisville, KY: Westminster John Knox Press, 2003.

Here, five Reformed theologians reflect on the prospects for Reformed theology in the third Christian millennium.

Gerrish, B. A. *Tradition and the Modern World: Reformed Theology in the Nineteenth Century.* Chicago: University of Chicago Press, 1978.

Gerrish, a leading Reformed historian and theologian, provides five essays on important nineteenth-century Reformed theologians and their relation to earlier Reformed theology.

Gordon, Bruce, and Carl R. Trueman, eds. *The Oxford Handbook of Calvin and Calvinism.* New York: Oxford University Press, 2021.

This major reference work presents thirty-nine scholarly essays that explore the historical development of Calvin's thought into Calvinism combining theology with cultural influences throughout the world.

Guthrie, Shirley C. *Always Being Reformed: Faith for a Fragmented World.* 2nd ed. Louisville, KY: Westminster John Knox Press, 2008.

Here a noted Reformed theologian reflects on aspects of Reformed theology in light of the fragmented contemporary world.

Hart, D. G. *Calvinism: A History.* New Haven, CT: Yale University Press, 2013.

This is a historical-theological study of Calvinism and its global spread.

Heppe, Heinrich. *Reformed Dogmatics Set Out and Illustrated from the Sources.* Rev. and ed. Ernst Bizer. Trans. G. T. Thomson. Rpt. Grand Rapids, MI: Baker Book House, 1978.

Heppe's book is a standard source book for quotations from major Reformed theologians on the twenty-eight theological doctrines.

Hesselink, I. John. *On Being Reformed: Distinctive Characteristics and Common Misunderstandings.* 2nd ed. New York: Reformed Church Press, 1988.

This is a helpful book for pastors and laity that addresses "misunderstandings" about Reformed theology and what it means to be "Reformed."

Leith, John H. *An Introduction to the Reformed Tradition.* Rev. ed. Atlanta: John Knox Press, 1981.

Leith provides a wide introduction to the Reformed tradition with important chapters on Reformed theology and its emphases.

McKim, Donald K., ed. *The Cambridge Companion to John Calvin.* New York: Cambridge University Press, 2004.

Here are scholarly essays that explore Calvin's theological thought and its development and appropriations in Reformed theology.

McKim, Donald K., ed. *Encyclopedia of the Reformed Faith*. Louisville, KY: Westminster John Knox Press, 1992.

This is a one-volume encyclopedia with major figures and topics of church history and theology being dealt with from a Reformed theological perspective. It is written by leading Reformed theologians.

McKim, Donald K. *Introducing the Reformed Faith: Biblical Revelation, Christian Tradition, Contemporary Significance*. Louisville, KY: Westminster John Knox Press, 2001.

McKim provides an introduction to Reformed theology and its doctrines with each presented in relation to Biblical Bases, Christian Tradition, Reformed Emphases, and Contemporary Significance.

McKim, Donald K., ed. *Major Themes in the Reformed Tradition*. Rpt. Eugene, OR: Wipf & Stock, 1998.

Here is a collection of thirty-seven important essays from a variety of Reformed theologians which present major dimensions of Reformed theology in seven categories.

McKim, Donald K. *More Presbyterian Questions, More Presbyterian Answers*. Rev. ed. Louisville, KY: Westminster John Knox Press, 2017.

This is a collection of theological questions and answers written from a Presbyterian perspective on Reformed theology.

McKim, Donald K. *Presbyterian Beliefs: A Brief Introduction*. Rev. ed. Louisville, KY: Westminster John Knox Press, 2017.

McKim provides a narrative discussion of major theological doctrines written from a Presbyterian perspective on Reformed theology.

McKim, Donald K. *Presbyterian Questions, Presbyterian Answers: Exploring Christian Faith*. Rev. ed. Louisville, KY: Westminster John Knox Press, 2017.

Here is a collection of theological questions and answers from a Presbyterian perspective on Reformed theology.

McKim, Donald K., ed. *Readings in Calvin's Theology*. Rpt. Eugene, OR: Wipf & Stock, 1998.

This is a collection of eighteen essays presenting Calvin's theological perspectives on major Christian doctrines.

McKim, Donald K., ed. *The Westminster Handbook to Reformed Theology*. The Westminster Handbooks to Christian Theology. Louisville, KY: Westminster John Knox Press, 2001.

This book collects the theological pieces from the *Encyclopedia of the Reformed Faith*.

McNeill, John T. *The History and Character of Calvinism*. New York: Oxford University Press, 1967.
McNeill's book is a classic discussion of the history and theology of Zwingli and Calvin and the spread of Reformed Protestantism in Europe and Early America.

Muller, Richard A. *Dictionary of Latin and Greek Theological Terms Drawn Principally from Protestant Scholastic Theology*. Grand Rapids, MI: Baker Book House, 1985; 2nd ed. 2017.
Muller's book is an indispensable guide to the intricacies of Reformed Orthodoxy and other Scholastic theologians through careful definitions and discussions of Latin and Greek theological terms.

Muller, Richard. A. *Post-Reformation Reformed Dogmatics*. 4 vols. Grand Rapids, MI: Baker, 2003.
This is an important presentation of Reformed theology as expressed in the writings of major Reformed Orthodox theologians in the seventeenth century.

Nimmo, Paul T., and David A. S. Fergusson, eds. *The Cambridge Companion to Reformed Theology*. New York: Cambridge University Press, 2016.
Here is a fine collection of Reformed scholars writing twenty essays on Reformed theology in relation to Theological Topics, Theological Figures, and Theological Contexts.

Osterhaven, M. Eugene. *The Faith of the Church: A Reformed Perspective on Its Historical Development*. Grand Rapids, MI: William B. Eerdmans, 1982.
Osterhaven provides a historical treatment of Christian doctrines as understood in Reformed theology that draws on the richness of the church's theological perspectives.

Presbyterian Church (USA). *Book of Confessions*. Study ed., rev. Louisville, KY: Westminster John Knox Press, 2017.
This collection of Confessional statements that form the doctrinal standards for the Presbyterian Church in the United States of America is a fine source for historic and contemporary Reformed theological statements of belief.

Rogers, Jack. *Presbyterian Creeds: A Guide to the Book of Confessions*. Louisville, KY: Westminster John Knox Press, 1991.
Rogers provides a guide to the theology and history of the confessions found in *The Book of Confessions* of the Presbyterian Church in the United States of America while also stressing their contemporary relevance.

Rohls, Jan. *Reformed Confessions: Theology from Zurich to Barmen*. Columbia Series in Reformed Theology. Louisville, KY: Westminster John Knox Press, 1998.

This is a theological discussion of important Reformed Confessions from the sixteenth to the twentieth century.

Selderhuis, Herman J., ed. *A Companion to Reformed Orthodoxy*. Brill's Companions to the Christian Tradition. Boston: Brill, 2013.

This is a valuable guide to the period of Reformed orthodoxy (1550–1750) in which Reformed theology became more systematized. Leading Reformed scholars provide essays on Relations, Places, and Topics. The essays are detailed and provide resources on important theologians and theological doctrines.

Selderhuis, Herman J., ed. *The Calvin Handbook*. Various translators. Grand Rapids, MI: William B. Eerdmans, 2009.

Here an international array of scholars presents entries on Calvin's life, theology, and the history of his reception. This is an important resource for the study of Reformed theology.

Smith, Gary Scott, and P. C. Kemeny, eds. *The Oxford Handbook of Presbyterianism*. New York: Oxford University Press, 2019.

This is a collection of thirty-five essays on the theology and other aspects of Presbyterianism as an expression of Reformed theology.

Torrance, Thomas F., ed. and trans. *The School of Faith: The Catechisms of the Reformed Church*. New York: Harper & Brothers, 1959.

Torrance provides a helpful collection of important historic Reformed catechisms.

Vischer, Lukas, ed. *Reformed Witness Today: A Collection of Confessions and Statements of Faith Issued by Reformed Churches*. Bern: Evangelische Arbeitsstelle Oekumene Schweiz, 1982.

This is a useful collection of Reformed theological Confessions and Statements of Faith from global Reformed churches.

Walker, Williston. *Creeds and Platforms of Congregationalism*. Rpt. New York: Pilgrim Press, 1991.

Walker's book is a classic study of theological documents from the Congregationalist branch of Reformed theology.

Willis, David, and Michael Welker, eds. *Toward the Future of Reformed Theology: Tasks, Topics, Traditions*. Grand Rapids, MI: William B. Eerdmans, 1999.

Here is a collection of thirty-one essays that examine the development of Reformed theology in diverse cultural, historical, and social contexts.

~

About the Author

Rev. Dr. Donald K. McKim is an Honorably Retired minister of the Presbyterian Church (U.S.A.). He has served as a pastor, seminary theology professor, and academic dean, as well as an editor for Westminster John Knox Press and Congregational Ministries Publishing. He is editor of *The Encyclopedia of the Reformed Faith* and author/editor of more than sixty books. Among his books are *Coffee with Calvin: Daily Devotions* and *Presbyterian Questions, Presbyterian Answers*.

Milton Keynes UK
Ingram Content Group UK Ltd.
UKHW011346220823
427290UK00015B/133